한국의 토익 수험자 여러분께,

토익 시험은 세계적인 직무 영어능력 평가 시험으로, 지난 40여 년간 비즈니스 현장에서 필요한 영어능력 평가의 기준을 제시해 왔습니다. 토익 시험 및 토익스피킹, 토익라이팅 시험은 세계에서 가장 널리 통용되는 영어능력 검증 시험으로, 160여 개국 14,000여 기관이 토익 성적을 의사결정에 활용하고 있습니다.

YBM은 한국의 토익 시험을 주관하는 ETS 독점 계약사입니다.

ETS는 한국 수험자들의 효과적인 토익 학습을 돕고자 YBM을 통하여 'ETS 토익 공식 교재'를 독점 출간하고 있습니다. 또한 'ETS 토익 공식 교재' 시리즈에 기출문항을 제공해 한국의 다른 교재들에 수록된 기출을 복제하거나 변형한 문항으로 인하여 발생할 수 있는 수험자들의 혼동을 방지하고 있습니다.

복제 및 변형 문항들은 토익 시험의 출제의도를 벗어날 수 있기 때문에 기출문항을 수록한 'ETS 토익 공식 교재'만큼 시험에 잘 대비할 수 없습니다.

'ETS 토익 공식 교재'를 통하여 수험자 여러분의 영어 소통을 위한 노력에 큰 성취가 있기를 바랍니다.

감사합니다.

Dear TOEIC Test Takers in Korea,

The TOEIC program is the global leader in English-language assessment for the workplace. It has set the standard for assessing English-language skills needed in the workplace for more than 40 years. The TOEIC tests are the most widely used English language assessments around the world, with 14,000+ organizations across more than 160 countries trusting TOEIC scores to make decisions.

YBM is the ETS Country Master Distributor for the TOEIC program in Korea and so is the exclusive distributor for TOEIC Korea.

To support effective learning for TOEIC test-takers in Korea, ETS has authorized YBM to publish the only Official TOEIC prep books in Korea. These books contain actual TOEIC items to help prevent confusion among Korean test-takers that might be caused by other prep book publishers' use of reproduced or paraphrased items.

Reproduced or paraphrased items may fail to reflect the intent of actual TOEIC items and so will not prepare test-takers as well as the actual items contained in the ETS TOEIC Official prep books published by YBM.

We hope that these ETS TOEIC Official prep books enable you, as test-takers, to achieve great success in your efforts to communicate effectively in English.

Thank you.

입문부터 실전까지 수준별 학습을 통해 최단기 목표점수 달성!

ETS TOEIC® 공식수험서
스마트 학습 지원

구글플레이, 앱스토어에서
ETS 토익기출 수험서 다운로드

구글플레이   앱스토어

ETS 토익 모바일 학습 플랫폼!

ETS® 토익기출 수험서 어플

교재 학습 지원
1. 교재 해설 강의
2. LC 음원 MP3
3. 교재/부록 모의고사 채점 및 분석
4. 단어 암기장

부가 서비스
1. 데일리 학습(토익 기출문제 풀이)
2. 토익 최신 경향 무료 특강
3. 토익 타이머

모의고사 결과 분석
1. 파트별/문항별 정답률
2. 파트별/유형별 취약점 리포트
3. 전체 응시자 점수 분포도

ETS TOEIC 공식카페 ▾

etstoeicbook.co.kr

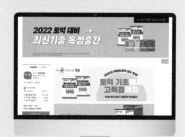

ETS 토익 학습 전용 온라인 커뮤니티!

ETS TOEIC® Book 공식카페

강사진의 학습 지원 토익 대표강사들의 학습 지원과 멘토링

교재 학습관 운영 교재별 학습게시판을 통해 무료 동영상 강의 등 학습 지원

학습 콘텐츠 제공 토익 학습 콘텐츠와 정기시험 예비특강 업데이트

---

www.ybmbooks.com에서도 무료 MP3를 다운로드 받을 수 있습니다.

ETS TOEIC

토익® 정기시험
기출문제집 2
1000
LISTENING

YBM

토익 정기시험
기출문제집 2
1000
LISTENING

발행인 허문호

발행처 YBM

편집 윤경림, 최정현, 이혜진, 허유정

디자인 이미화, 이현숙

마케팅 정연철, 박천산, 고영노, 박찬경, 김동진, 김윤하

초판발행 2019년 12월 16일

17쇄발행 2023년 8월 1일

신고일자 1964년 3월 28일

신고번호 제 300-1964-3호

주소 서울시 종로구 종로 104

전화 (02) 2000-0515 [구입문의] / (02) 2000-0345 [내용문의]

팩스 (02) 2285-1523

홈페이지 www.ybmbooks.com

ISBN 978-89-17-23218-9

토익® 정기시험
기출문제집 2
1000
LISTENING

Preface

Dear test taker,

English-language proficiency has become a vital tool for success. It can help you excel in business, travel the world, and communicate effectively with friends and colleagues. The TOEIC® test measures your ability to function effectively in English in these types of situations. Because TOEIC scores are recognized around the world as evidence of your English-language proficiency, you will be able to confidently demonstrate your English skills to employers and begin your journey to success.

The test developers at ETS are excited to help you achieve your personal and professional goals through the use of the ETS® TOEIC® 정기시험 기출문제집 1000 Vol. 2. This book contains test questions taken from actual, official TOEIC tests. They will help you become familiar with the TOEIC test's format and content. This book also contains detailed explanations of the question types and language points contained in the TOEIC test. These test questions and explanations have all been prepared by the same test specialists who develop the actual TOEIC test, so you can be confident that you will receive an authentic test-preparation experience.

Features of the ETS® TOEIC® 정기시험 기출문제집 1000 Vol. 2 include the following.

- Ten full-length test forms, all accompanied by answer keys and official scripts
- Specific and easy to understand explanations for learners
- The very same ETS voice actors that you will hear in an official TOEIC test administration

---

By using the ETS® TOEIC® 정기시험 기출문제집 1000 Vol. 2 to prepare for the TOEIC test, you can be assured that you have a professionally prepared resource that will provide you with accurate guidance so that you are more familiar with the tasks, content, and format of the test and that will help you maximize your TOEIC test score. With your official TOEIC score certificate, you will be ready to show the world what you know!

We are delighted to assist you on your TOEIC journey with the ETS® TOEIC® 정기시험 기출문제집 1000 Vol. 2 and wish you the best of success.

최신 기출문제 전격 공개!

'출제기관이 독점 제공한' 기출문제가 담긴 유일한 교재!

이 책에는 정기시험 기출문제 10세트가 수록되어 있다. 최신 기출문제로 실전 감각을 키워 시험에
확실하게 대비하자!

'정기시험 성우 음성'으로 실전 대비!

이 책에 수록된 10세트의 LC 음원은 모두 실제 시험에서 나온 정기 시험 성우의 음원이다.
시험장에서 듣게 될 음성으로 공부하면 까다로운 영국·호주식 발음도 걱정 없다.

'ETS가 제공하는' 표준점수 환산표!

출제기관 ETS가 독점 제공하는 표준점수 환산표를 수록했다. 채점 후 환산표를 통해
자신의 실력이 어느 정도인지 가늠해 보자!

What is the TOEIC?

TOEIC은 어떤 시험인가요?

Test of English for International Communication(국제적 의사소통을 위한 영어 시험)의 약자로서, 영어가 모국어가 아닌 사람들이 일상생활 또는 비즈니스 현장에서 꼭 필요한 실용적 영어 구사 능력을 갖추었는가를 평가하는 시험이다.

시험 구성

구성	Part	내용		문항수	시간	배점
듣기(L/C)	1	사진 묘사		6	45분	495점
	2	질의 & 응답		25		
	3	짧은 대화		39		
	4	짧은 담화		30		
읽기(R/C)	5	단문 빈칸 채우기(문법/어휘)		30	75분	495점
	6	장문 빈칸 채우기		16		
	7	독해	단일 지문	29		
			이중 지문	10		
			삼중 지문	15		
Total	7 Parts			200문항	120분	990점

TOEIC 접수는 어떻게 하나요?

TOEIC 접수는 한국 토익 위원회 사이트(www.toeic.co.kr)에서 온라인 상으로만 접수가 가능하다. 사이트에서 매월 자세한 접수 일정과 시험 일정 등의 구체적 정보 확인이 가능하니, 미리 일정을 확인하여 접수하도록 한다.

시험장에 반드시
가져가야 할 준비물은요?

신분증 규정 신분증만 가능

(주민등록증, 운전면허증, 기간 만료 전의 여권, 공무원증 등)

필기구 연필, 지우개 (볼펜이나 사인펜은 사용 금지)

시험은 어떻게
진행되나요?

09:20	입실 (09:50 이후는 입실 불가)
09:30 – 09:45	답안지 작성에 관한 오리엔테이션
09:45 – 09:50	휴식
09:50 – 10:05	신분증 확인
10:05 – 10:10	문제지 배부 및 파본 확인
10:10 – 10:55	듣기 평가 (Listening Test)
10:55 – 12:10	독해 평가 (Reading Test)

TOEIC 성적 확인은
어떻게 하죠?

시험일로부터 약 10~11일 후, 인터넷과 ARS(060-800-0515)로 성적을 확인할 수 있다. TOEIC 성적표는 우편이나 온라인으로 발급 받을 수 있다(시험 접수시, 양자 택일). 우편으로 발급 받을 경우는 성적 발표 후 대략 일주일이 소요되며, 온라인 발급을 선택하면 유효기간 내에 홈페이지에서 본인이 직접 1회에 한해 무료 출력할 수 있다. TOEIC 성적은 시험일로부터 2년간 유효하다.

TOEIC은
몇 점 만점인가요?

TOEIC 점수는 듣기 영역(LC) 점수, 읽기 영역(RC) 점수, 그리고 이 두 영역을 합계한 전체 점수 세 부분으로 구성된다. 각 부분의 점수는 5점 단위이며, 5점에서 495점에 걸쳐 주어지고, 전체 점수는 10점에서 990점까지이며, 만점은 990점이나. TOEIC 성적은 각 문제 유형의 난이도에 따른 점수 환산표에 의해 결정된다.

토익 경향 분석

1인 등장 사진
주어는 He/She, A man/woman 등이며 주로 앞부분에 나온다.

2인 이상 등장 사진
주어는 They, Some men/women/people,
One of the men/women 등이며 주로 중간 부분에 나온다.

사물/배경 사진
주어는 A car, Some chairs 등이며 주로 뒷부분에 나온다.

사람 또는 사물 중심 사진
주어가 일부는 사람, 일부는 사물이며 주로 뒷부분에 나온다.

사람 또는
사물 중심 사진
33%

1인
등장 사진
33%

**PART 1
최신 출제 경향**

사물/
배경 사진
17%

2인 이상
등장 사진
17%

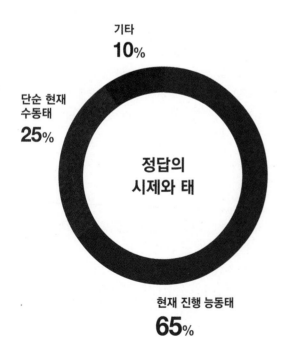

기타
10%

단순 현재
수동태
25%

**정답의
시제와 태**

현재 진행 능동태
65%

현재 진행 능동태
〈is/are + 현재분사〉 형태이며 주로 사람이 주어이다.

단순 현재 수동태
〈is/are + 과거분사〉 형태이며 주로 사물이 주어이다.

기타
〈is/are + being + 과거분사〉 형태의 현재 진행 수동태, 〈has/ have + been + 과거 분사〉 형태의 현재 완료 수동태, '타동사 + 목적어' 형태의 단순 현재 능동태, There is/are와 같은 단순 현재도 나온다.

평서문
질문이 아니라 객관적인 사실이나 화자의 의견
등을 나타내는 문장이다.

명령문
동사원형이나 Please 등으로 시작한다.

의문사 의문문
각 의문사마다 1~2개씩 나온다. 의문사가 단
독으로 나오기도 하지만 What time ~?, How
long ~?, Which room ~? 등에서처럼 다른 명
사나 형용사와 같이 나오기도 한다.

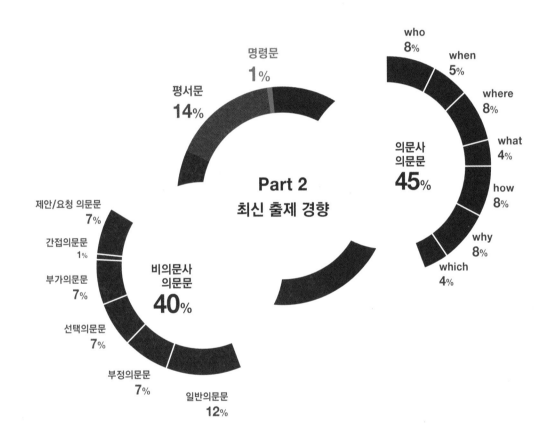

비의문사 의문문
일반(Yes/No) 의문문 적게 나올 때는 한두 개, 많이 나올 때는 서너 개씩 나오는 편이다.
부정의문문 Don't you ~?, Isn't he ~? 등으로 시작하는 문장이며 일반 긍정 의문문보다는 약간 더 적게 나온다.
선택의문문 A or B 형태로 나오며 A와 B의 형태가 단어, 구, 절일 수 있다. 구나 절일 경우 문장이 길어져서 어려워진다.
부가의문문 ~ don't you?, ~ isn't he? 등으로 끝나는 문장이며, 일반 부정 의문문과 비슷하다고 볼 수 있다.
간접의문문 의문사가 문장 처음 부분이 아니라 문장 중간에 들어 있다.
제안/요청 의문문 정보를 얻기보다는 상대방의 도움이나 동의 등을 얻기 위한 목적이 일반적이다.

토익 경향 분석

PART 3	짧은 대화 Short Conversations	총 13대화문 39문제 (지문당 3문제)

- 3인 대화의 경우 남자 화자 두 명과 여자 화자 한 명 또는 남자 화자 한 명과 여자 화자 두 명이 나온다. 따라서 문제에서는 2인 대화에서와 달리 the man이나 the woman이 아니라 the men이나 the women 또는 특정한 이름이 언급될 수 있다.

- 대화 & 시각 정보는 항상 파트의 뒷부분에 나온다.

- 시각 성보의 유형으로 chart, map, floor plan, schedule, table, weather forecast, directory, list, invoice, receipt, sign, packing slip 등 다양한 자료가 골고루 나온다.

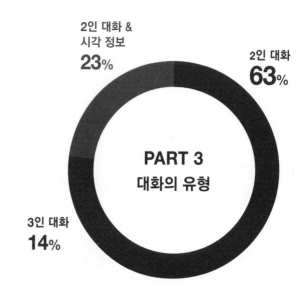

2인 대화 & 시각 정보 **23%**

2인 대화 **63%**

3인 대화 **14%**

PART 3 대화의 유형

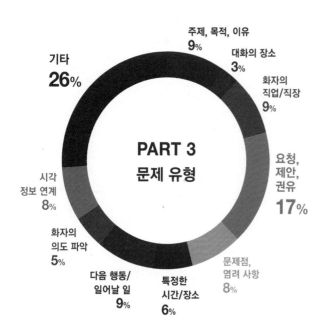

주제, 목적, 이유 **9%**

대화의 장소 **3%**

화자의 직업/직장 **9%**

요청, 제안, 권유 **17%**

문제점, 염려 사항 **8%**

특정한 시간/장소 **6%**

다음 행동/ 일어날 일 **9%**

화자의 의도 파악 **5%**

시각 정보 연계 **8%**

기타 **26%**

PART 3 문제 유형

- 주제, 목적, 이유, 대화의 장소, 화자의 직업/직장 등과 관련된 문제는 주로 대화의 첫 번째 문제로 나오며 다음 행동/일어날 일 등과 관련된 문제는 주로 대화의 세 번째 문제로 나온다.

- 화자의 의도 파악 문제는 주로 2인 대화에 나오지만, 가끔 3인 대화에 나오기도 한다. 시각 정보 연계 대화에는 나오지 않고 있다.

- Part 3 안에서 화자의 의도 파악 문제는 2개가 나오고 시각 정보 연계 문제는 3개가 나온다.

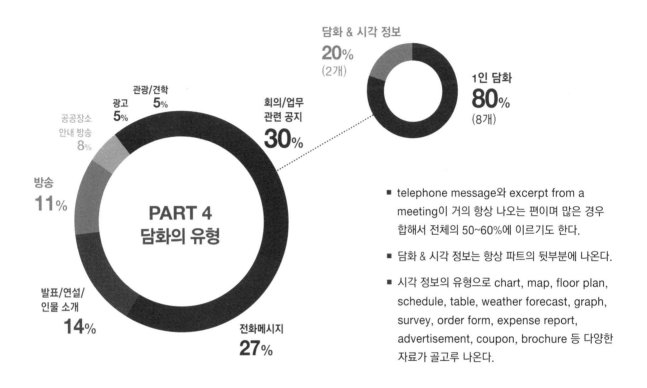

PART 4
담화의 유형

담화 & 시각 정보
20%
(2개)

1인 담화
80%
(8개)

회의/업무
관련 공지
30%

관광/견학 **5**%
광고 **5**%
공공장소 안내 방송 **8**%
방송 **11**%
발표/연설/인물 소개 **14**%
전화메시지 **27**%

- telephone message와 excerpt from a meeting이 거의 항상 나오는 편이며 많은 경우 합해서 전체의 50~60%에 이르기도 한다.

- 담화 & 시각 정보는 항상 파트의 뒷부분에 나온다.

- 시각 정보의 유형으로 chart, map, floor plan, schedule, table, weather forecast, graph, survey, order form, expense report, advertisement, coupon, brochure 등 다양한 자료가 골고루 나온다.

- 문제 유형은 기본적으로 Part 3과 거의 비슷하다.

- 주제, 목적, 이유, 담화의 장소, 화자의 직업/직장 등과 관련된 문제는 주로 담화의 첫 번째 문제로 나오며 다음 행동/일어날 일 등과 관련된 문제는 주로 담화의 세 번째 문제로 나온다.

- Part 4 안에서 화자의 의도 파악 문제는 3개가 나오고 시각 정보 연계 문제는 2개가 나온다.

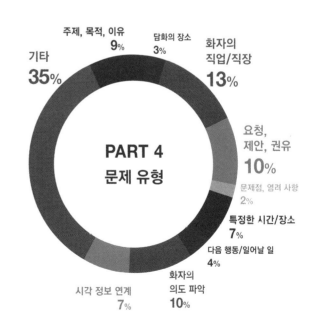

PART 4
문제 유형

주제, 목적, 이유 **9**%
담화의 장소 **3**%
화자의 직업/직장 **13**%
기타 **35**%
요청, 제안, 권유 **10**%
문제점, 염려 사항 **2**%
특정한 시간/장소 **7**%
다음 행동/일어날 일 **4**%
화자의 의도 파악 **10**%
시각 정보 연계 **7**%

PART 5 단문 빈칸 채우기 Incomplete Sentences | 총 30문제

문법 문제

시제와 대명사와 관련된 문법 문제가 2개씩,
한정사와 분사와 관련된 문법 문제가 1개씩
나온다. 시제 문제의 경우 능동태/수동태나
수의 일치와 연계되기도 한다. 그 밖에 한정사,
능동태/수동태, 부정사, 동명사 등과 관련된
문법 문제가 나온다.

어휘 문제

동사, 명사, 형용사, 부사와 관련된 어휘
문제가 각각 2~3개씩 골고루 나온다.
전치사 어휘 문제는 3개씩 꾸준히
나오지만, 접속사나 어구와 관련된 어휘
문제는 나오지 않을 때도 있고 3개가
나올 때도 있다.

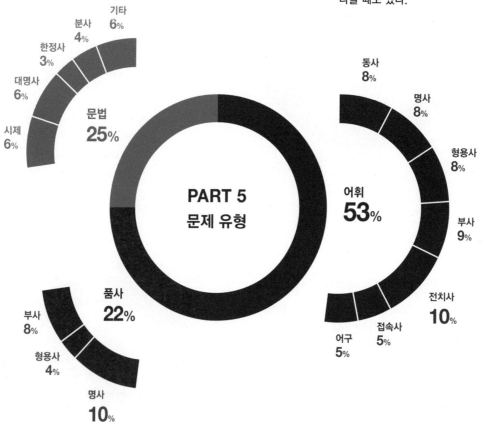

품사 문제

명사와 부사와 관련된 품사 문제가
2~3개씩 나오며, 형용사와 관련된 품사
문제가 상대적으로 적은 편이다.

한 지문에 4문제가 나오며 평균적으로 어휘 문제가 2개, 품사나
문법 문제가 1개, 문맥에 맞는 문장 고르기 문제가 1개 들어간다.
문맥에 맞는 문장 고르기 문제를 제외하면 문제 유형은 기본적
으로 파트 5와 거의 비슷하다.

어휘 문제
동사, 명사, 부사, 어구와 관련된 어휘 문제는
매번 1~2개씩 나온다. 부사 어휘 문제의 경우
therefore(그러므로)나 however(하지만)처럼
문맥의 흐름을 자연스럽게 연결해 주는 부사가 자주
나온다.

문맥에 맞는 문장 고르기
문맥에 맞는 문장 고르기 문제는 지문당 한 문제씩
나오는데, 나오는 위치의 확률은 4문제 중 두 번째
문제, 세 번째 문제, 네 번째 문제, 첫 번째 문제
순으로 높다.

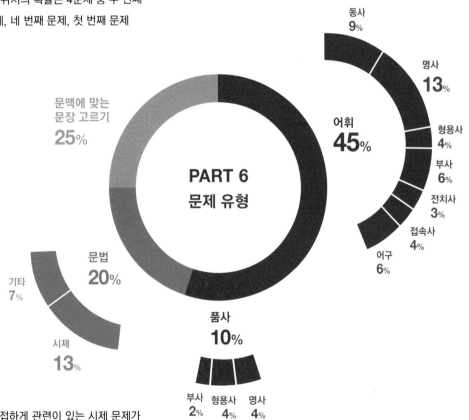

문법 문제
문맥의 흐름과 밀접하게 관련이 있는 시제 문제가
2개 정도 나오며, 능동태/수동태나 수의 일치와
연계되기도 한다. 그 밖에 대명사, 능동태/수동태,
부정사, 접속사/전치사 등과 관련된 문법 문제가
나온다.

품사 문제
명사나 형용사 문제가 부사 문제보다 좀 더
자주 나온다.

PART 7 독해 Reading Comprehension

지문 유형	지문당 문제 수	지문 개수	비중 %
단일 지문	2문항	4개	약 15%
	3문항	3개	약 16%
	4문항	3개	약 22%
이중 지문	5문항	2개	약 19%
삼중 지문	5문항	3개	약 28%

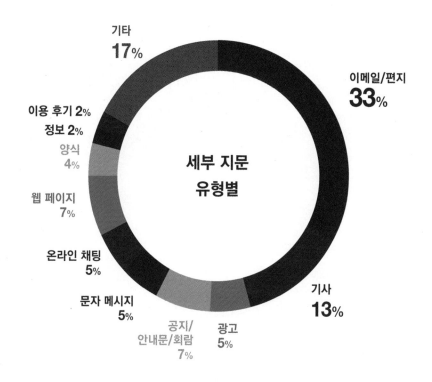

세부 지문 유형별

- 기타 17%
- 이메일/편지 33%
- 이용 후기 2%
- 정보 2%
- 양식 4%
- 웹 페이지 7%
- 온라인 채팅 5%
- 문자 메시지 5%
- 공지/안내문/회람 7%
- 광고 5%
- 기사 13%

■ 이메일/편지, 기사 유형 지문은 거의 항상 나오는 편이며 많은 경우 합해서 전체의 50~60%에 이르기도 한다.

■ 기타 지문 유형으로 agenda, brochure, comment card, coupon, flyer, instructions, invitation, invoice, list, menu, page from a catalog, policy statement, report, schedule, survey, voucher 등 다양한 자료가 골고루 나온다.

(이중 지문과 삼중 지문 속의 지문들을 모두 낱개로 계산함 – 총 23지문)

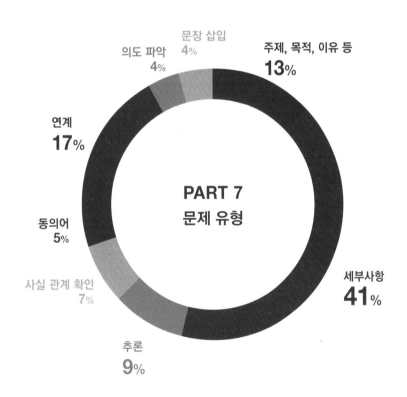

■ 동의어 문제는 주로 이중 지문이나 삼중 지문에 나온다.
■ 연계 문제는 일반적으로 이중 지문에서 한 문제, 삼중 지문에서 두 문제가 나온다.
■ 의도 파악 문제는 문자 메시지(text-message chain)나 온라인 채팅(online chat discussion) 지문에서 출제되며 두 문제가
  나온다.
■ 문장 삽입 분제는 주로 기사, 이메일, 편지, 회람 지문에서 출제되며 두 문제가 나온다.

점수 환산표 및 산출법

점수 환산표   이 책에 수록된 각 Test를 풀고 난 후, 맞은 개수를 세어 점수를 환산해 보세요.

LISTENING Raw Score (맞은 개수)	LISTENING Scaled Score (환산 점수)	READING Raw Score (맞은 개수)	READING Scaled Score (환산 점수)
96-100	475-495	96-100	460-495
91-95	435-495	91-95	425-490
86-90	405-470	86-90	400-465
81-85	370-450	81-85	375-440
76-80	345-420	76-80	340-415
71-75	320-390	71-75	310-390
66-70	290-360	66-70	285-370
61-65	265-335	61-65	255-340
56-60	240-310	56-60	230-310
51-55	215-280	51-55	200-275
46-50	190-255	46-50	170-245
41-45	160-230	41-45	140-215
36-40	130-205	36-40	115-180
31-35	105-175	31-35	95-150
26-30	85-145	26-30	75-120
21-25	60-115	21-25	60-95
16-20	30-90	16-20	45-75
11-15	5-70	11-15	30-55
6-10	5-60	6-10	10-40
1-5	5-50	1-5	5-30
0	5-35	0	5-15

점수 산출 방법
아래의 방식으로 점수를 산출할 수 있다.

자신의 답안을 수록된 정답과 대조하여 채점한다. 각 Section의 맞은 개수가 본인의 Section별 '실제 점수 (통계 처리하기 전의 점수, raw score)'이다. Listening Test와 Reading Test의 정답 수를 세어, 자신의 실제 점수를 아래의 해당란에 기록한다.

	맞은 개수	환산 점수대
LISTENING		
READING		
총점		

Section별 실제 점수가 그대로 Section별 TOEIC 점수가 되는 것은 아니다. TOEIC은 시행할 때마다 별도로 특정한 통계 처리 방법을 사용하며 이러한 실제 점수를 환산 점수(converted[scaled] score)로 전환하게 된다. 이렇게 전환함으로써, 매번 시행될 때마다 문제는 달라지지만 그 점수가 갖는 의미는 같아지게 된다. 예를 들어 어느 한 시험에서 총점 550점의 성적으로 받는 실력이라면 다른 시험에서도 거의 550점대의 성적을 받게 되는 것이다.

▼

실제 점수를 위 표에 기록한 후 왼쪽 페이지의 점수 환산표를 보도록 한다. TOEIC이 시행될 때마다 대개 이와 비슷한 형태의 표가 작성되는데, 여기 제시된 환산표는 본 교재에 수록된 Test용으로 개발된 것이다. 이 표를 사용하여 자신의 실제 점수를 환산 점수로 전환하도록 한다. 즉, 예를 들어 Listening Test의 실제 정답 수가 61~65개이면 환산 점수는 265점에서 335점 사이가 된다. 여기서 실제 정답 수가 61개이면 환산 점수가 265점이고, 65개이면 환산 점수가 335점 임을 의미하는 것은 아니다. 본 책의 Test를 위해 작성된 이 점수 환산표가 자신의 영어 실력이 어느 정도인지 대략적으로 파악하는 데 도움이 되긴 하지만, 이 표가 실제 TOEIC 성적 산출에 그대로 사용된 적은 없다는 사실을 밝혀 둔다.

토익 정기시험
기출문제집

LC

기출 TEST

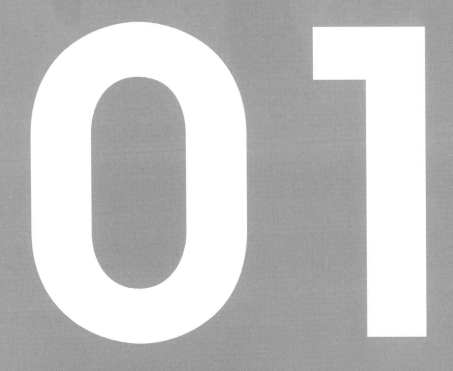

01

LISTENING TEST

In the Listening test, you will be asked to demonstrate how well you understand spoken English. The entire Listening test will last approximately 45 minutes. There are four parts, and directions are given for each part. You must mark your answers on the separate answer sheet. Do not write your answers in your test book.

PART 1

Directions: For each question in this part, you will hear four statements about a picture in your test book. When you hear the statements, you must select the one statement that best describes what you see in the picture. Then find the number of the question on your answer sheet and mark your answer. The statements will not be printed in your test book and will be spoken only one time.

Statement (C), "They're sitting at a table," is the best description of the picture, so you should select answer (C) and mark it on your answer sheet.

1.

2.

GO ON TO THE NEXT PAGE

3.

4.

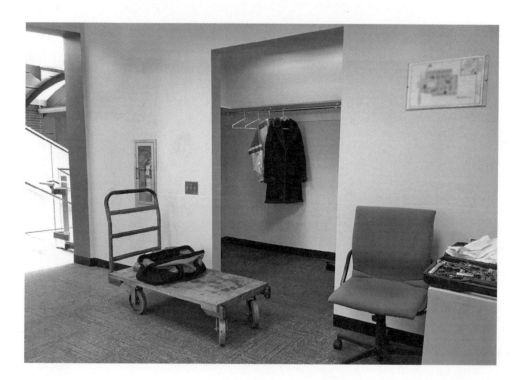

5.

6.

GO ON TO THE NEXT PAGE

PART 2

Directions: You will hear a question or statement and three responses spoken in English. They will not be printed in your test book and will be spoken only one time. Select the best response to the question or statement and mark the letter (A), (B), or (C) on your answer sheet.

7. Mark your answer on your answer sheet.

8. Mark your answer on your answer sheet.

9. Mark your answer on your answer sheet.

10. Mark your answer on your answer sheet.

11. Mark your answer on your answer sheet.

12. Mark your answer on your answer sheet.

13. Mark your answer on your answer sheet.

14. Mark your answer on your answer sheet.

15. Mark your answer on your answer sheet.

16. Mark your answer on your answer sheet.

17. Mark your answer on your answer sheet.

18. Mark your answer on your answer sheet.

19. Mark your answer on your answer sheet.

20. Mark your answer on your answer sheet.

21. Mark your answer on your answer sheet.

22. Mark your answer on your answer sheet.

23. Mark your answer on your answer sheet.

24. Mark your answer on your answer sheet.

25. Mark your answer on your answer sheet.

26. Mark your answer on your answer sheet.

27. Mark your answer on your answer sheet.

28. Mark your answer on your answer sheet.

29. Mark your answer on your answer sheet.

30. Mark your answer on your answer sheet.

31. Mark your answer on your answer sheet.

PART 3

Directions: You will hear some conversations between two or more people. You will be asked to answer three questions about what the speakers say in each conversation. Select the best response to each question and mark the letter (A), (B), (C), or (D) on your answer sheet. The conversations will not be printed in your test book and will be spoken only one time.

32. Where is the conversation most likely taking place?

    (A) At a hardware store
    (B) At a clothing shop
    (C) At a bakery
    (D) At a pharmacy

33. How do the speakers hope to increase sales?

    (A) By advertising online
    (B) By offering a new product
    (C) By providing free delivery
    (D) By discounting some items

34. What will the man do next?

    (A) Contact a vendor
    (B) Talk to a colleague
    (C) File some invoices
    (D) Get some more supplies

35. What does the woman say a town recently did?

    (A) It elected a mayor.
    (B) It fixed a train line.
    (C) It cleaned up a community park.
    (D) It added a bicycle lane.

36. Why is the woman pleased about a change?

    (A) Her monthly bills are lower.
    (B) Her commute is quicker.
    (C) Recycling is easier.
    (D) A neighborhood looks nicer.

37. What does the man suggest the woman do?

    (A) Join a club
    (B) Enter a competition
    (C) Check an agenda
    (D) Post a review

38. What type of company do the men work for?

    (A) An architectural firm
    (B) An engineering firm
    (C) A construction company
    (D) An electronics manufacturer

39. What is the purpose of the telephone call?

    (A) To cancel an order
    (B) To arrange an interview
    (C) To ask about a policy
    (D) To confirm a reservation

40. What will be sent to the woman?

    (A) A magazine article
    (B) A warranty
    (C) Directions to a location
    (D) Instructions for refunds

41. Where does the man work?

    (A) At a bus station
    (B) At a financial firm
    (C) At a dental office
    (D) At an auto repair shop

42. What does the man offer to contact the woman about?

    (A) A business's holiday hours
    (B) An appointment opening
    (C) The status of a delivery
    (D) The cost of a service

43. Why does the man say, "the Number 10 bus stops right outside our building"?

    (A) To recommend that the woman take the bus
    (B) To request that a bus route be extended
    (C) To correct an error on a map
    (D) To complain about traffic noise

44. Where are the speakers?

(A) At a department store
(B) At a medical clinic
(C) At a library
(D) At a bank

45. What is the woman trying to do?

(A) Pick up a prescription
(B) Join a rewards program
(C) Make a deposit
(D) Borrow a book

46. What will the man do next?

(A) Speak to a manager
(B) Prepare some forms
(C) Refund a purchase
(D) Upgrade some software

47. What product are the distributors coming to see?

(A) A vehicle
(B) A mobile phone
(C) A computer desk
(D) A refrigerator

48. Why has the meeting been rescheduled?

(A) Some materials did not arrive.
(B) Some employees are still training.
(C) A flight was delayed.
(D) A room was not available.

49. What will the woman do next?

(A) Call a car service
(B) Submit some paperwork
(C) Hire some caterers
(D) Inspect some equipment

50. Where are the speakers?

(A) At a conference
(B) At a factory tour
(C) At an interview
(D) At a laboratory

51. What does the man say he wants to do?

(A) Take some pictures
(B) Ask a question
(C) Look at some machinery
(D) Review a slide show

52. What does the woman remind the man to do?

(A) Send a résumé
(B) Pay a fee
(C) Choose an item
(D) Enjoy some refreshments

53. What business is the man calling from?

(A) An architectural firm
(B) A marketing agency
(C) An electronics store
(D) A printing shop

54. Why does the woman say, "We actually have a new company logo"?

(A) To compliment a colleague
(B) To reassure a client
(C) To request an update to an order
(D) To express surprise at a decision

55. What does the woman ask the man to do?

(A) Charge a credit card
(B) Obtain a supervisor's approval
(C) Close an account
(D) Update a contract

56. What do the women do at the museum?

(A) Manage the gift shop
(B) Lead tours
(C) Collect donations
(D) Restore paintings

57. What most likely caused an increase in museum visitors?

(A) Free parking
(B) Extended hours of operation
(C) A new exhibit
(D) Lower ticket prices

58. According to the man, what will happen on Thursday?

(A) A film will be shown.
(B) An article will be published.
(C) A city official will host a fund-raiser.
(D) An art collector will give a talk.

---

59. What problem does the man have?

(A) He was overcharged for a service.
(B) He forgot his password.
(C) His computer has not been delivered.
(D) His computer is not working properly.

60. What did the man's purchase include?

(A) A screen protector
(B) A carrying case
(C) Technical support
(D) Virus protection

61. What information does the woman request?

(A) A phone number
(B) A mailing address
(C) A model number
(D) A purchase date

Menu Options

Stuffed Eggplant	$6 per person
Vegetable Pasta	$8 per person
Roast Chicken	$10 per person
Baked Salmon	$12 per person

62. What are the speakers preparing for?

(A) A job fair
(B) A client visit
(C) A training session
(D) A retirement dinner

63. Look at the graphic. How much will the speakers most likely spend per person?

(A) $6
(B) $8
(C) $10
(D) $12

64. What does the woman say she will do next?

(A) Prepare an itinerary
(B) Buy some train passes
(C) Visit some restaurants
(D) Confirm a hotel reservation

GO ON TO THE NEXT PAGE

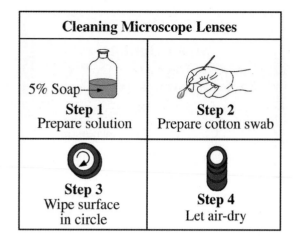

Cleaning Microscope Lenses

5% Soap→ **Step 1** Prepare solution	**Step 2** Prepare cotton swab
Step 3 Wipe surface in circle	**Step 4** Let air-dry

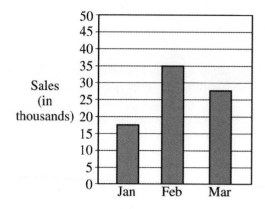

Sales (in thousands)

65. Why does the woman want to talk to the man?

(A) To ask for some advice
(B) To discuss a complaint
(C) To explain a schedule change
(D) To decline an invitation

66. Look at the graphic. Which step in the procedure does the woman mention?

(A) Step 1
(B) Step 2
(C) Step 3
(D) Step 4

67. What does the woman say she will do?

(A) Post some instructions
(B) Put away some equipment
(C) Write a report
(D) Forward an e-mail

68. Where do the speakers most likely work?

(A) At a hardware store
(B) At a driving school
(C) At an automotive supply company
(D) At an international shipping company

69. Look at the graphic. Which month's sales figures does the woman ask about?

(A) January
(B) February
(C) March
(D) April

70. What does the man say they will do this month?

(A) Launch a new marketing campaign
(B) Offer a discount for bulk purchases
(C) Hire a consultant
(D) Increase production

PART 4

Directions: You will hear some talks given by a single speaker. You will be asked to answer three questions about what the speaker says in each talk. Select the best response to each question and mark the letter (A), (B), (C), or (D) on your answer sheet. The talks will not be printed in your test book and will be spoken only one time.

71. According to the speaker, what will take place on Saturday?

    (A) A retirement party
    (B) A holiday parade
    (C) A business workshop
    (D) A company picnic

72. Where do the listeners work?

    (A) At a bank
    (B) At an amusement park
    (C) At a restaurant
    (D) At a police station

73. What does the speaker suggest that the listeners do?

    (A) Wear warm clothing
    (B) Use public transportation
    (C) Pack a lunch
    (D) Bring identification

74. Where does the speaker most likely work?

    (A) At an advertising agency
    (B) At a technology firm
    (C) At an art museum
    (D) At an electronics store

75. What is the talk mainly about?

    (A) Updating a logo
    (B) Changing a display
    (C) Organizing a contest
    (D) Offering a seminar

76. What does the speaker say he will do this morning?

    (A) Set up a meeting
    (B) Submit a supply order
    (C) Update a Web site
    (D) Print some posters

77. What is the speaker mainly discussing?

    (A) A computer program
    (B) A conveyor belt
    (C) A storage space
    (D) A cooling fan

78. What key difference does the speaker point out?

    (A) Some machinery will run faster.
    (B) Some alarms are more sensitive.
    (C) A password has been changed.
    (D) A time sheet is online.

79. What does the speaker say the listeners must do?

    (A) Speak with a supervisor
    (B) Sign a document
    (C) Watch a video
    (D) Work extra hours

80. According to the speaker, what will happen on Wednesday?

    (A) A career fair
    (B) A promotional sale
    (C) A work site inspection
    (D) An employee orientation

81. What does the speaker imply when she says, "I don't have any appointments tomorrow"?

    (A) She has not been successful with a client.
    (B) She thinks a schedule is wrong.
    (C) She has time to take over a task.
    (D) She needs to leave work early.

82. What does the speaker ask the listener to do?

    (A) Call her back
    (B) Check a calendar
    (C) Reserve a booth
    (D) Cancel an event

GO ON TO THE NEXT PAGE

83. According to the speaker, what is special about this month's issue of *Tech Now*?

    (A) It is free for university students.
    (B) It is about women in technology.
    (C) It is the magazine's first issue.
    (D) It has a reader survey.

84. Who is Erika Cliffton?

    (A) A company's founder
    (B) A journalist
    (C) An athlete
    (D) A financial consultant

85. What does the magazine offer this week with a subscription?

    (A) A laptop case
    (B) An umbrella
    (C) Access to job listings
    (D) A discount coupon for a store

86. What is the broadcast mainly about?

    (A) Diet advice
    (B) Exercise tips
    (C) Improving sleep
    (D) Reducing stress

87. Why does the speaker say she is surprised?

    (A) A task can be very time-consuming.
    (B) A popular view is incorrect.
    (C) A local business is closing.
    (D) A speaker is arriving late.

88. Why does the speaker say, "We'll be talking about that on next week's broadcast"?

    (A) To change a schedule
    (B) To make a complaint
    (C) To refuse a request
    (D) To publicize a future episode

89. According to the speaker, what is unique about the airport?

    (A) It will be powered by solar energy.
    (B) It will be made from recycled materials.
    (C) It will be built by a famous architect.
    (D) It will be the largest in the country.

90. What does the speaker say will happen next month?

    (A) A board meeting
    (B) A training session
    (C) A job fair
    (D) A grand opening

91. According to the speaker, how can the listeners get information about the construction firm?

    (A) By dialing a toll-free number
    (B) By visiting a Web site
    (C) By watching a documentary
    (D) By picking up a brochure

92. What is the topic of this week's podcast?

    (A) Historical monuments
    (B) Some missing paintings
    (C) Classical literature
    (D) European composers

93. Who is the guest on this week's podcast?

    (A) An actor
    (B) A travel agent
    (C) A politician
    (D) A professor

94. Why does the speaker say, "this program is only made possible by the financial support of our members"?

    (A) To encourage the listeners to make a donation
    (B) To apologize for a limited number of episodes
    (C) To prevent people from getting a bonus
    (D) To express concern about a proposal

Job-Seeker Workshops

June 3	Research job market
June 10	Dress for success
June 17	Practice interviews
June 24	After the interview

Community Garden

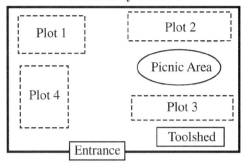

95. Look at the graphic. On which date is the talk being given?

(A) June 3
(B) June 10
(C) June 17
(D) June 24

96. What will the listeners do after the break?

(A) Answer survey questions
(B) Participate in group work
(C) Review some résumés
(D) Watch a video

97. What does the speaker remind the listeners about?

(A) Some research questions
(B) Some schedule changes
(C) A payment method
(D) A sign-in sheet

98. Who is the speaker?

(A) A security guard
(B) A project coordinator
(C) A course instructor
(D) A news journalist

99. Look at the graphic. Where will herbs be planted?

(A) Plot 1
(B) Plot 2
(C) Plot 3
(D) Plot 4

100. What does the speaker plan to do on Saturday?

(A) Lead a tour
(B) Attend a picnic
(C) Take some photographs
(D) Install a fence

This is the end of the Listening test.

토익˚정기시험
기출문제집

LC

기출 TEST

02

LISTENING TEST

In the Listening test, you will be asked to demonstrate how well you understand spoken English. The entire Listening test will last approximately 45 minutes. There are four parts, and directions are given for each part. You must mark your answers on the separate answer sheet. Do not write your answers in your test book.

PART 1

Directions: For each question in this part, you will hear four statements about a picture in your test book. When you hear the statements, you must select the one statement that best describes what you see in the picture. Then find the number of the question on your answer sheet and mark your answer. The statements will not be printed in your test book and will be spoken only one time.

Statement (C), "They're sitting at a table," is the best description of the picture, so you should select answer (C) and mark it on your answer sheet.

1.

2.

GO ON TO THE NEXT PAGE

3.

4.

5.

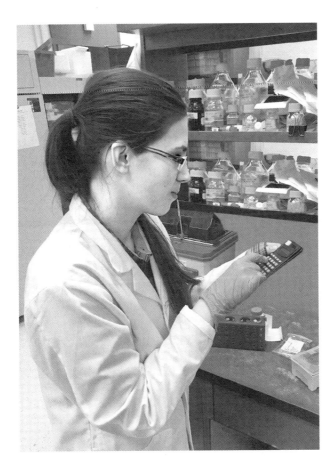

6.

GO ON TO THE NEXT PAGE ➤

TEST **2**

PART 2

Directions: You will hear a question or statement and three responses spoken in English. They will not be printed in your test book and will be spoken only one time. Select the best response to the question or statement and mark the letter (A), (B), or (C) on your answer sheet.

7. Mark your answer on your answer sheet.

8. Mark your answer on your answer sheet.

9. Mark your answer on your answer sheet.

10. Mark your answer on your answer sheet.

11. Mark your answer on your answer sheet.

12. Mark your answer on your answer sheet.

13. Mark your answer on your answer sheet.

14. Mark your answer on your answer sheet.

15. Mark your answer on your answer sheet.

16. Mark your answer on your answer sheet.

17. Mark your answer on your answer sheet.

18. Mark your answer on your answer sheet.

19. Mark your answer on your answer sheet.

20. Mark your answer on your answer sheet.

21. Mark your answer on your answer sheet.

22. Mark your answer on your answer sheet.

23. Mark your answer on your answer sheet.

24. Mark your answer on your answer sheet.

25. Mark your answer on your answer sheet.

26. Mark your answer on your answer sheet.

27. Mark your answer on your answer sheet.

28. Mark your answer on your answer sheet.

29. Mark your answer on your answer sheet.

30. Mark your answer on your answer sheet.

31. Mark your answer on your answer sheet.

PART 3

Directions: You will hear some conversations between two or more people. You will be asked to answer three questions about what the speakers say in each conversation. Select the best response to each question and mark the letter (A), (B), (C), or (D) on your answer sheet. The conversations will not be printed in your test book and will be spoken only one time.

32. Who is Mr. Benson?

    (A) An assistant
    (B) A client
    (C) A project manager
    (D) A shipping coordinator

33. Why did Mr. Benson call?

    (A) To request an earlier delivery
    (B) To inquire about a bill
    (C) To report a mistake
    (D) To complain about some noise

34. What does the woman say she will do?

    (A) Place an order
    (B) Change suppliers
    (C) Collect some tools
    (D) Review some blueprints

35. What is taking place tomorrow?

    (A) A cooking class
    (B) A grand opening
    (C) A company dinner
    (D) A music festival

36. What does the woman hope will happen?

    (A) A job will become available.
    (B) An event will begin on time.
    (C) Store sales will increase.
    (D) Tourism to an area will improve.

37. What does the man say he will do next?

    (A) Print out some coupons
    (B) Design a flyer
    (C) Decorate a room
    (D) Stock some shelves

38. According to the speakers, what happened last week?

    (A) A new product was launched.
    (B) A software package was purchased.
    (C) A technical issue was resolved.
    (D) A regional office was closed.

39. What industry do the speakers work in?

    (A) Health care
    (B) Finance
    (C) Technology
    (D) Education

40. What will the man do next week?

    (A) Attend a training
    (B) Travel for business
    (C) Prepare a slideshow
    (D) Revise a contract

41. Where do the speakers work?

    (A) At a bank
    (B) At a coffee shop
    (C) At a bookstore
    (D) At a medical clinic

42. Why is the woman concerned?

    (A) Her inventory is low.
    (B) She lost some contact information.
    (C) A seating area is too cold.
    (D) Road construction is disruptive.

43. What does the man imply when he says, "I used to work at a hardware store"?

    (A) He can fix a problem.
    (B) He has experience in customer service.
    (C) He is not interested in an offer.
    (D) He is excited about teaching a new course.

GO ON TO THE NEXT PAGE

44. What product are the speakers discussing?

(A) A camera
(B) A printer
(C) A television
(D) A mobile phone

45. What problem does the woman mention?

(A) An item is damaged.
(B) An item is out of stock.
(C) A display price is incorrect.
(D) A delivery was not received.

46. What does the manager offer the woman?

(A) A refund
(B) An extended warranty
(C) Free membership
(D) Express shipping

47. Where does the conversation most likely take place?

(A) At a drug store
(B) At a fitness center
(C) At a research laboratory
(D) At a dentist's office

48. What does the man give to the woman?

(A) A toothbrush
(B) A pamphlet
(C) A water bottle
(D) A receipt

49. What does the man ask the woman to do?

(A) Pay a fee
(B) Sign a form
(C) Provide an address
(D) Make an appointment

50. What type of business does the woman work for?

(A) A grocery store
(B) A publishing company
(C) A marketing firm
(D) A travel agency

51. What does the woman mean when she says, "we'd really like to fill the position this week"?

(A) A candidate should decide quickly.
(B) An alternative plan needs to be approved.
(C) Additional funding will be required.
(D) A manager will change a timeline.

52. According to the woman, what does the company always pay for?

(A) Housing
(B) Equipment
(C) Clothing
(D) Transportation

53. What are the speakers mainly talking about?

(A) A holiday parade
(B) A charity event
(C) A health seminar
(D) A company picnic

54. What does Amelia offer to do tomorrow?

(A) Speak with some colleagues
(B) Pick up some supplies
(C) Finalize a travel itinerary
(D) Contact a news reporter

55. Why will the man be in Washington?

(A) To inspect a building
(B) To accept an award
(C) To attend a conference
(D) To interview for a job

56. Where do the speakers most likely work?

(A) At a shoe store
(B) At a furniture store
(C) At an auto repair shop
(D) At a kitchen appliance store

57. Why does the man decline the woman's request at first?

(A) He is on a short break.
(B) He is preparing a display.
(C) He is about to leave work.
(D) He is assisting another client.

58. What does the man say about an item?

(A) It is broken.
(B) It is discounted.
(C) It is easy to operate.
(D) It is probably unavailable.

59. Why is the man calling?

(A) To conduct a survey
(B) To inquire about a convention
(C) To provide some feedback
(D) To promote a product

60. What does the woman say she is interested in?

(A) Making online payments
(B) Buying a membership
(C) Reducing energy costs
(D) Funding a research project

61. What does the woman request?

(A) A demonstration
(B) A site visit
(C) A registration form
(D) A financing plan

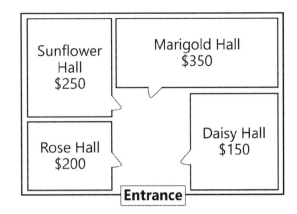

62. What event is the man calling about?

(A) A trade show
(B) A training workshop
(C) An awards dinner
(D) A retirement celebration

63. Look at the graphic. How much will the man's reservation cost?

(A) $200
(B) $250
(C) $350
(D) $150

64. According to the woman, why is a catering business popular?

(A) It offers vegetarian dishes.
(B) It uses local ingredients.
(C) The prices are reasonable.
(D) The chef is famous.

GO ON TO THE NEXT PAGE

Factory Productivity
Lightbulbs Produced per Month

Interview Process

Step 1   Computer-skills test
Step 2   Phone conversation
Step 3   Group interview
Step 4   On-site interview

65. What will the speakers do this afternoon?

(A) Order replacement parts
(B) Lead a staff meeting
(C) Host a client lunch
(D) Conduct a facility tour

66. Look at the graphic. Which month do the speakers agree to discuss?

(A) March
(B) April
(C) May
(D) June

67. What does the woman suggest doing?

(A) Improving security
(B) Hiring qualified employees
(C) Building another warehouse
(D) Inspecting some machines

68. According to the woman, what is the benefit of changing a process?

(A) It will decrease the workload.
(B) It will make the company more competitive.
(C) It will help prevent mistakes.
(D) It will save money.

69. Look at the graphic. Which step do the speakers agree should be removed?

(A) Step 1
(B) Step 2
(C) Step 3
(D) Step 4

70. What will the speakers do next?

(A) Review a budget
(B) Prepare a presentation
(C) Print out some résumés
(D) Hire a consultant

PART 4

Directions: You will hear some talks given by a single speaker. You will be asked to answer three questions about what the speaker says in each talk. Select the best response to each question and mark the letter (A), (B), (C), or (D) on your answer sheet. The talks will not be printed in your test book and will be spoken only one time.

71. What event is the speaker mainly talking about?

(A) A sports competition
(B) A grand opening
(C) A nutrition workshop
(D) A community festival

72. What are the listeners encouraged to do during the event?

(A) Sample different foods
(B) Watch a demonstration
(C) Purchase souvenirs
(D) Take pictures

73. What can the listeners find on a Web site?

(A) A list of sponsors
(B) Information about parking
(C) Some contest guidelines
(D) Some membership options

74. Where most likely does this announcement take place?

(A) At a ferry terminal
(B) At an airport
(C) At a train station
(D) At a travel agency

75. According to the speaker, what can the listeners do for free?

(A) Check extra luggage
(B) Change a seat assignment
(C) Order a meal
(D) Take a map

76. What does the speaker ask the listeners to do?

(A) Look at a ticket
(B) Change a reservation
(C) Stand in a line
(D) Provide some identification

77. Who most likely is the speaker?

(A) A tour guide
(B) A chef
(C) A taxi driver
(D) A politician

78. According to the speaker, what is special about Rosedale's city hall?

(A) Its age
(B) Its location
(C) Its architecture
(D) Its size

79. Why does the speaker say, "the bus leaves at 3:00 P.M."?

(A) He is unhappy with an itinerary.
(B) He cannot accept an invitation.
(C) He wants the listeners to be on time.
(D) He thinks the listeners should use other transportation.

80. What is the purpose of the meeting?

(A) To delegate projects
(B) To introduce a client
(C) To organize a seminar
(D) To present survey results

81. What is the main complaint about a phone application?

(A) It is slow.
(B) It is unattractive.
(C) It is hard to use.
(D) It has high fees.

82. What will happen next?

(A) Lunch will be delivered.
(B) A schedule will be finalized.
(C) A consultant will make a presentation.
(D) Team members will test a new product.

GO ON TO THE NEXT PAGE

83. Where do the listeners work?

(A) At a bank
(B) At a restaurant
(C) At a sports arena
(D) At a construction company

84. What does the speaker imply when she says, "our business is increasing"?

(A) A marketing campaign has been successful.
(B) The local population has grown.
(C) An additional branch will be opened.
(D) More employees will be hired.

85. What does the speaker offer the listeners?

(A) A higher salary
(B) Reserved parking spaces
(C) Free festival tickets
(D) Discount meal coupons

86. What does the speaker's company mainly sell?

(A) Gardening equipment
(B) Computer accessories
(C) Stationery supplies
(D) Home furniture

87. How has the company addressed a problem?

(A) By opening more stores
(B) By lowering prices
(C) By updating a product line
(D) By merging with another company

88. What does the speaker ask the listeners to do?

(A) Prepare a press release
(B) Revise some designs
(C) Review a financial forecast
(D) Speak to customers

89. What is the main purpose of the message?

(A) To give feedback on some work
(B) To file a complaint
(C) To schedule an orientation
(D) To propose an idea for a new product

90. What problem does the speaker mention?

(A) A deadline has passed.
(B) A road is closed.
(C) A machine is out of order.
(D) A report is missing.

91. What does the speaker say the listener can do during lunch?

(A) Ask questions
(B) Make a telephone call
(C) Sign some paperwork
(D) Pick up a photo ID

92. Where do the listeners most likely work?

(A) At an art gallery
(B) At a fitness center
(C) At a department store
(D) At an advertising agency

93. What will the company do?

(A) Require some training
(B) Invest in a system upgrade
(C) Pay for some classes
(D) Add some vacation days

94. Why does the speaker say, "it has earned many awards"?

(A) To explain a policy
(B) To make a recommendation
(C) To offer congratulations
(D) To correct a mistake

★ ★ ★ ★ ★ ★ ★ ★ ★ ★ ★		
Palden Movie Palace		
Stars on Mars	4:00	Theater 1
Long Distance Run	4:30	Theater 2
Manchester Tea Room	5:30	Theater 3
The Successful Apprentice	6:00	Theater 4

95. Why is the speaker calling?

(A) To ask about a lost item
(B) To confirm a schedule
(C) To complain about a service
(D) To cancel a reservation

96. Look at the graphic. Which theater was the speaker in yesterday?

(A) Theater 1
(B) Theater 2
(C) Theater 3
(D) Theater 4

97. What does the speaker request?

(A) A phone call
(B) A seat change
(C) A printed receipt
(D) A cash refund

Delville Shopping Complex: Layout

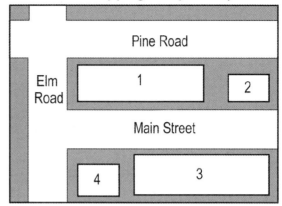

98. Who most likely are the listeners?

(A) Gardeners
(B) Security guards
(C) Sales clerks
(D) Postal workers

99. Look at the graphic. Which building does the speaker talk about?

(A) Building 1
(B) Building 2
(C) Building 3
(D) Building 4

100. What will the listeners most likely do next?

(A) Complete some paperwork
(B) Try on some uniforms
(C) Visit a work site
(D) Take a lunch break

This is the end of the Listening test.

토익˚ 정기시험
기출문제집

LC

기출 TEST

03

LISTENING TEST

In the Listening test, you will be asked to demonstrate how well you understand spoken English. The entire Listening test will last approximately 45 minutes. There are four parts, and directions are given for each part. You must mark your answers on the separate answer sheet. Do not write your answers in your test book.

PART 1

Directions: For each question in this part, you will hear four statements about a picture in your test book. When you hear the statements, you must select the one statement that best describes what you see in the picture. Then find the number of the question on your answer sheet and mark your answer. The statements will not be printed in your test book and will be spoken only one time.

Statement (C), "They're sitting at a table," is the best description of the picture, so you should select answer (C) and mark it on your answer sheet.

1.

2

GO ON TO THE NEXT PAGE ➤

3.

4.

5.

6.

GO ON TO THE NEXT PAGE

PART 2

Directions: You will hear a question or statement and three responses spoken in English. They will not be printed in your test book and will be spoken only one time. Select the best response to the question or statement and mark the letter (A), (B), or (C) on your answer sheet.

7. Mark your answer on your answer sheet.

8. Mark your answer on your answer sheet.

9. Mark your answer on your answer sheet.

10. Mark your answer on your answer sheet.

11. Mark your answer on your answer sheet.

12. Mark your answer on your answer sheet.

13. Mark your answer on your answer sheet.

14. Mark your answer on your answer sheet.

15. Mark your answer on your answer sheet.

16. Mark your answer on your answer sheet.

17. Mark your answer on your answer sheet.

18. Mark your answer on your answer sheet.

19. Mark your answer on your answer sheet.

20. Mark your answer on your answer sheet.

21. Mark your answer on your answer sheet.

22. Mark your answer on your answer sheet.

23. Mark your answer on your answer sheet.

24. Mark your answer on your answer sheet.

25. Mark your answer on your answer sheet.

26. Mark your answer on your answer sheet.

27. Mark your answer on your answer sheet.

28. Mark your answer on your answer sheet.

29. Mark your answer on your answer sheet.

30. Mark your answer on your answer sheet.

31. Mark your answer on your answer sheet.

PART 3

Directions: You will hear some conversations between two or more people. You will be asked to answer three questions about what the speakers say in each conversation. Select the best response to each question and mark the letter (A), (B), (C), or (D) on your answer sheet. The conversations will not be printed in your test book and will be spoken only one time.

32. Where does the woman work?

    (A) At an electronics store
    (B) At a newspaper publisher
    (C) At a bank
    (D) At a hotel

33. Why is the man calling?

    (A) To update a mailing address
    (B) To complain about a billing error
    (C) To inquire about a job opening
    (D) To request a price estimate

34. What does the woman say she will do next?

    (A) Schedule an appointment
    (B) Talk to a coworker
    (C) Process a refund
    (D) Send some samples

35. What are the speakers preparing for?

    (A) A training session
    (B) A marketing presentation
    (C) An employee celebration
    (D) A board meeting

36. What problem does the man mention?

    (A) A computer is not working.
    (B) A staff member is unavailable.
    (C) A document is incorrect.
    (D) A door is locked.

37. What does the woman ask the man to do?

    (A) Create name tags
    (B) Set up some equipment
    (C) Clean a conference room
    (D) Confirm a supply order

38. Where does the man work?

    (A) At a travel agency
    (B) At a theater
    (C) At a museum
    (D) At a fitness center

39. What is the reason for the call?

    (A) A payment is late.
    (B) An event has been canceled.
    (C) A reservation is incomplete.
    (D) An offer will expire.

40. What does the man say he will e-mail to the woman?

    (A) A brochure
    (B) A survey
    (C) A sales receipt
    (D) A discount code

41. What are the speakers planning?

    (A) A client visit
    (B) A health fair
    (C) A fund-raising dinner
    (D) A company outing

42. What does the woman mean when she says, "we've done that for three years in a row"?

    (A) She does not have much experience with a task.
    (B) She thinks an activity has been popular.
    (C) She does not want to repeat an activity.
    (D) She does not need directions to a location.

43. What does the man say he is concerned about?

    (A) The price of a class
    (B) The distance to a venue
    (C) Road closures
    (D) Scheduling conflicts

GO ON TO THE NEXT PAGE

44. Who most likely are the women?

    (A) Athletes
    (B) Musicians
    (C) Radio announcers
    (D) Clothing manufacturers

45. What do the women want to hire the man to do?

    (A) Design some merchandise
    (B) Repair some equipment
    (C) Plan some events
    (D) Move some furniture

46. What does the man request from the women?

    (A) A reimbursement
    (B) An official certificate
    (C) A contract signature
    (D) A completed questionnaire

47. How did the woman learn about a company's products?

    (A) She saw an advertisement.
    (B) She heard about them from a neighbor.
    (C) She is a regular customer.
    (D) She lives near the store.

48. What does the man mention about the product?

    (A) It is inexpensive.
    (B) It is easy to install.
    (C) It decreases water use.
    (D) It is available in many colors.

49. What does the woman ask the man to do?

    (A) E-mail more information
    (B) Provide a cost estimate
    (C) Schedule a delivery
    (D) Call back later

50. Who most likely is the man?

    (A) A librarian
    (B) A teacher
    (C) A news reporter
    (D) A local politician

51. What does the woman like best about the new library building?

    (A) Its modern appearance
    (B) Its convenient location
    (C) Its operating hours
    (D) Its large book collection

52. What benefit will library members have?

    (A) Free parking
    (B) Discounts on special classes
    (C) Access to electronic books
    (D) Tickets to local museums

53. Why did the man go to the store?

    (A) To meet a friend
    (B) To return a purchase
    (C) To pick up an order
    (D) To join a rewards program

54. What problem does the salesperson have?

    (A) She forgot her computer password.
    (B) She needs to leave work early.
    (C) She lost her identification badge.
    (D) She is not familiar with a procedure.

55. What does the manager ask the man for?

    (A) A telephone number
    (B) A receipt
    (C) A credit card
    (D) A shipping address

56. What project is the man working on?

(A) Updating a Web site
(B) Editing a catalog
(C) Organizing a company banquet
(D) Writing a magazine article

57. What does the woman suggest changing?

(A) A company logo
(B) A project deadline
(C) Some prices
(D) Some photographs

58. What does the man say he will do?

(A) Contact some colleagues
(B) Review an inventory report
(C) Borrow some equipment
(D) Check a company handbook

59. Where do the speakers most likely work?

(A) At a department store
(B) At an accounting firm
(C) At a law firm
(D) At an advertising agency

60. Why does the man say, "Marius Cosmetics was my first account here"?

(A) To show that he understands a problem
(B) To explain that he no longer works with a client
(C) To complain about a coworker's mistake
(D) To request a promotion

61. What does the man suggest doing?

(A) Rejecting a proposal
(B) Getting help from a manager
(C) Preparing some samples
(D) Revising a budget

Nearby Restaurants

* Nico's Italian Trattoria
  31 Orwell Blvd.

* Kim's Korean Grill
  22 Main St.

* Ana's Steakhouse
  76 Rose Ave.

* Aruna's Indian Buffet
  48 Lord St.

62. What field do the speakers most likely work in?

(A) Technology
(B) Journalism
(C) Medicine
(D) Agriculture

63. What will take place in the afternoon?

(A) An interview
(B) A workshop
(C) A job fair
(D) A trade show

64. Look at the graphic. Where will the speakers probably have lunch?

(A) At Nico's Italian Trattoria
(B) At Kim's Korean Grill
(C) At Ana's Steakhouse
(D) At Aruna's Indian Buffet

GO ON TO THE NEXT PAGE

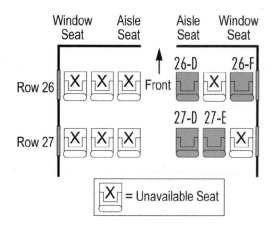

Window Seat | Aisle Seat | Aisle Seat | Window Seat

Row 26 — 26-D 26-F

Row 27 — 27-D 27-E

Front

X = Unavailable Seat

Open interview times:

Tuesday	9 A.M.
Wednesday	Noon
Thursday	4 P.M.
Friday	2 P.M.

65. What is the purpose of the woman's trip?

(A) To attend a conference
(B) To take a vacation
(C) To meet with some potential clients
(D) To assist with a branch opening

66. What does the woman agree to do?

(A) Give a presentation
(B) Pay an additional fee
(C) Travel on a different day
(D) Make a dinner reservation

67. Look at the graphic. Which seat does the woman request?

(A) 26D
(B) 26F
(C) 27D
(D) 27E

68. What kind of experience does the man say he has?

(A) Advertising
(B) Customer service
(C) Delivery driving
(D) Marketing

69. Look at the graphic. Which day will the man be interviewed?

(A) On Tuesday
(B) On Wednesday
(C) On Thursday
(D) On Friday

70. According to the woman, what should the man bring to the interview?

(A) A list of references
(B) A professional certificate
(C) A photo ID
(D) A printed application

PART 4

Directions: You will hear some talks given by a single speaker. You will be asked to answer three questions about what the speaker says in each talk. Select the best response to each question and mark the letter (A), (B), (C), or (D) on your answer sheet. The talks will not be printed in your test book and will be spoken only one time.

71. Why are some colleagues visiting the company?

(A) To inspect a facility
(B) To celebrate an anniversary
(C) To make a presentation
(D) To participate in a training

72. What are the listeners asked to volunteer to do?

(A) Give a city tour
(B) Arrange transportation
(C) Prepare some documents
(D) Contact a catering service

73. What are volunteers asked to send in an e-mail?

(A) Their qualifications
(B) Their availability
(C) Contact information
(D) A list of supplies

74. Where does the announcement most likely take place?

(A) At a train station
(B) At a taxi stand
(C) At a ferry terminal
(D) At an airport

75. According to the speaker, what has been changed?

(A) A boarding time
(B) A refund policy
(C) A departure gate
(D) A trip route

76. What does the speaker say the listeners must show?

(A) Proof of payment
(B) Photo identification
(C) A credit card
(D) An itinerary

77. What is the main topic of the report?

(A) Community activities
(B) Traffic updates
(C) Business tips
(D) Entertainment news

78. What does the speaker recommend that the listeners do?

(A) Fill out a survey
(B) Attend a town meeting
(C) Check a map
(D) Drive slowly

79. What does the speaker say will happen next week?

(A) A prize will be given.
(B) A construction project will start.
(C) A company office will open.
(D) A government official will be interviewed.

80. Where most likely are the listeners?

(A) On a bus
(B) On a boat
(C) At a museum
(D) At a library

81. According to the speaker, what will the listeners be able to see?

(A) Local markets
(B) Unusual wildlife
(C) Historic buildings
(D) Famous artwork

82. What does the speaker imply when he says, "We'll be coming back the opposite way on the return trip"?

(A) The listeners will be able to take pictures.
(B) There was an error in a travel itinerary.
(C) The listeners can use some lockers.
(D) The listeners should buy souvenirs.

GO ON TO THE NEXT PAGE

83. What good news does the speaker share?

(A) A contract was renewed.
(B) A deadline was extended.
(C) A new employee was hired.
(D) A larger building was purchased.

84. What kind of business does the speaker work for?

(A) An automobile factory
(B) A landscape service
(C) A book printing company
(D) A dry cleaning service

85. What does the speaker mean when he says, "I've already called the manufacturer"?

(A) He expects sales to increase.
(B) He has extra time to help.
(C) He has reassigned a task.
(D) He is addressing a complaint.

86. What does the speaker's company sell?

(A) Packaged foods
(B) Agricultural equipment
(C) Home electronics
(D) Travel insurance

87. According to the speaker, what will happen next Friday?

(A) A potential client will visit.
(B) A language course will begin.
(C) A computer system will be installed.
(D) Some construction will be completed.

88. What does the speaker ask the listener to do?

(A) Reserve a table
(B) Notify a supervisor
(C) Pick up a vehicle
(D) Hire an interpreter

89. Where most likely are the listeners?

(A) At a professional conference
(B) At a career fair
(C) At a board meeting
(D) At a community festival

90. What will Dr. Jimenez talk about?

(A) Workplace safety
(B) Corporate investments
(C) Productivity and time management
(D) Personality traits and success

91. According to the speaker, what should the listeners do by the end of the month?

(A) Register for an event
(B) Submit a time sheet
(C) Sign a card
(D) Read a publication

92. Where does the speaker work?

(A) At a national park
(B) At a science museum
(C) At a university
(D) At a public library

93. What does the speaker imply when he says, "the seating area is almost full"?

(A) More chairs are needed.
(B) Some people cannot attend an event.
(C) A fund-raising goal was reached.
(D) A lecture is popular.

94. What does the speaker ask the listeners to do?

(A) Raise their hand to ask questions
(B) Turn off their mobile phones
(C) Stay in a designated area
(D) Refer to a map

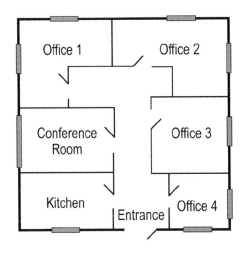

Gino's Restaurant	
Weekend Specials Menu	
Friday dinner:	Pizza with fresh tomatoes
Saturday lunch:	Pasta with red sauce
Saturday dinner:	Broiled fish with vegetables
Sunday lunch:	Grilled chicken with salad

95. Which department does the speaker most likely work in?

(A) Customer service
(B) Product development
(C) Maintenance
(D) Shipping

96. Why does the speaker want to meet with the listener?

(A) To make an introduction
(B) To handle a complaint
(C) To discuss a project
(D) To sign a contract

97. Look at the graphic. Which is the speaker's office?

(A) Office 1
(B) Office 2
(C) Office 3
(D) Office 4

98. Who are the listeners?

(A) Cooks
(B) Managers
(C) Food distributors
(D) Safety inspectors

99. Look at the graphic. What menu item will need to be replaced?

(A) Pizza
(B) Pasta
(C) Broiled fish
(D) Grilled chicken

100. What does the speaker want the listeners to do by 4:00 P.M. today?

(A) Prepare for an inspection
(B) E-mail some suggestions
(C) Arrange a delivery
(D) Print a new menu

This is the end of the Listening test.

토익˚ 정기시험
기출문제집

LC

기출 TEST

04

LISTENING TEST

In the Listening test, you will be asked to demonstrate how well you understand spoken English. The entire Listening test will last approximately 45 minutes. There are four parts, and directions are given for each part. You must mark your answers on the separate answer sheet. Do not write your answers in your test book.

PART 1

Directions: For each question in this part, you will hear four statements about a picture in your test book. When you hear the statements, you must select the one statement that best describes what you see in the picture. Then find the number of the question on your answer sheet and mark your answer. The statements will not be printed in your test book and will be spoken only one time.

Statement (C), "They're sitting at a table," is the best description of the picture, so you should select answer (C) and mark it on your answer sheet.

1.

2.

3.

4.

5.

6.

GO ON TO THE NEXT PAGE ➤

PART 2

Directions: You will hear a question or statement and three responses spoken in English. They will not be printed in your test book and will be spoken only one time. Select the best response to the question or statement and mark the letter (A), (B), or (C) on your answer sheet.

7. Mark your answer on your answer sheet.

8. Mark your answer on your answer sheet.

9. Mark your answer on your answer sheet.

10. Mark your answer on your answer sheet.

11. Mark your answer on your answer sheet.

12. Mark your answer on your answer sheet.

13. Mark your answer on your answer sheet.

14. Mark your answer on your answer sheet.

15. Mark your answer on your answer sheet.

16. Mark your answer on your answer sheet.

17. Mark your answer on your answer sheet.

18. Mark your answer on your answer sheet.

19. Mark your answer on your answer sheet.

20. Mark your answer on your answer sheet.

21. Mark your answer on your answer sheet.

22. Mark your answer on your answer sheet.

23. Mark your answer on your answer sheet.

24. Mark your answer on your answer sheet.

25. Mark your answer on your answer sheet.

26. Mark your answer on your answer sheet.

27. Mark your answer on your answer sheet.

28. Mark your answer on your answer sheet.

29. Mark your answer on your answer sheet.

30. Mark your answer on your answer sheet.

31. Mark your answer on your answer sheet.

PART 3

Directions: You will hear some conversations between two or more people. You will be asked to answer three questions about what the speakers say in each conversation. Select the best response to each question and mark the letter (A), (B), (C), or (D) on your answer sheet. The conversations will not be printed in your test book and will be spoken only one time.

32. Where most likely are the speakers?

(A) At an airport
(B) At an office building
(C) At a shopping center
(D) At a hotel

33. What was the woman unable to do this morning?

(A) Open a door
(B) Make photocopies
(C) Find a taxi
(D) Process a payment

34. What does the woman like about the man's suggestion?

(A) It accommodates her schedule.
(B) It is affordable.
(C) It will help increase sales.
(D) It will reduce commuting time.

35. What are the speakers getting ready for?

(A) A holiday season
(B) A corporate visit
(C) A renovation project
(D) A company picnic

36. What new feature will the supermarket introduce?

(A) A cooking class
(B) A gift-wrapping station
(C) A delivery service
(D) A special phone line

37. What will the man most likely do next?

(A) Pay some bills
(B) Create a calendar
(C) Talk to some colleagues
(D) Reply to an e-mail

38. What does the woman want to do?

(A) Replace an appliance
(B) Plant a garden
(C) Repair a floor
(D) Paint a wall

39. Why does the man recommend Kilgore products?

(A) They are easy to use.
(B) They are long lasting.
(C) They come with a warranty.
(D) They are safe for the environment.

40. What does the man offer to do?

(A) Demonstrate a product
(B) Contact a manufacturer
(C) Look for a contractor
(D) Provide some color samples

41. Why did the man call?

(A) To discuss an advertising strategy
(B) To inquire about a loan
(C) To request legal assistance
(D) To update contact information

42. What type of company is the man planning to purchase?

(A) An accounting firm
(B) A bookstore
(C) A travel agency
(D) A coffee shop

43. Why does the man ask for an online meeting?

(A) He will be out of town.
(B) His car is not working.
(C) Business hours are inconvenient.
(D) A location is difficult to find.

GO ON TO THE NEXT PAGE

44. Where are the speakers?

(A) At a hospital
(B) At a restaurant
(C) At a factory
(D) At a grocery store

45. Where will the speakers go later that day?

(A) To a conference room
(B) To a warehouse
(C) To a security office
(D) To a fitness center

46. What does the woman ask about?

(A) What the safety procedures are
(B) When a work schedule will be posted
(C) How to operate a machine
(D) Where to park a vehicle

47. What are the speakers discussing?

(A) Some broken locks
(B) Some missing equipment
(C) A department purchase
(D) A floor plan

48. Which department does the man most likely work in?

(A) Human Resources
(B) Legal
(C) Maintenance
(D) Sales

49. What does the woman imply when she says, "I was there this morning"?

(A) A schedule will be revised.
(B) A problem was not resolved.
(C) An explanation is not necessary.
(D) An appointment ended early.

50. What did a company recently do?

(A) It hired a new executive.
(B) It renewed a contract.
(C) It expanded its cafeteria menu.
(D) It ordered new furniture.

51. According to the women, what is the benefit of a change?

(A) It will be good for employee health.
(B) It will lead to staff promotions.
(C) It will lower production costs.
(D) It will enlarge some office space.

52. What do the women ask the man about?

(A) A budget
(B) A delivery date
(C) A seminar
(D) An upcoming holiday

53. What information does the woman ask the man for?

(A) Who is scheduled to work
(B) Why a job candidate was not hired
(C) What topic was discussed at a meeting
(D) When a shipment will arrive

54. What will happen next month?

(A) A software update will be released.
(B) A newsletter will be published.
(C) Salary increases will take effect.
(D) Some construction will begin.

55. What will the man e-mail to the woman?

(A) A spreadsheet of pay scales
(B) A signed contract
(C) Some designs for a brochure
(D) Some slides from a presentation

56. Why does the woman say, "It's not on Thursday"?

(A) To indicate relief
(B) To request an extension
(C) To confirm availability
(D) To express surprise

57. What problem does the woman mention?

(A) She cannot access some data.
(B) She did not receive a travel reimbursement.
(C) A client is unavailable.
(D) Transportation is unreliable.

58. What does the man say he will do?

(A) Check a reservation
(B) Contact a coworker
(C) Print out a form
(D) Review a document

---

59. Where do the speakers work?

(A) At an art supply store
(B) At a movie theater
(C) At a technology company
(D) At a jewelry store

60. What is the woman's main responsibility?

(A) Creating inventory lists
(B) Recruiting temporary help
(C) Making online videos
(D) Installing equipment

61. What does the woman ask the man to do?

(A) Edit a report
(B) Give some feedback
(C) Upload some pictures
(D) Open an account

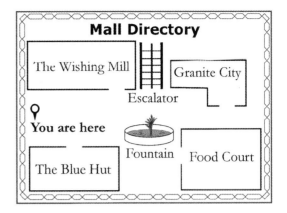

62. What does the woman want to do?

(A) Have an item repaired
(B) Return a product
(C) Eat a meal
(D) Apply for a job

63. Look at the graphic. Where will the woman most likely go next?

(A) The Wishing Mill
(B) Granite City
(C) Food Court
(D) The Blue Hut

64. What does the man remind the woman about?

(A) A discount has ended.
(B) An escalator is not working.
(C) A restaurant has limited seating.
(D) A mall is closing soon.

TEST 4

GO ON TO THE NEXT PAGE

Regular Tickets:
–$10

Discounted Tickets:
–$5 on Mondays
–$3 after 5 P.M.
–$2 for students
and members

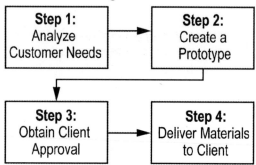

Design Process

Step 1: Analyze Customer Needs	Step 2: Create a Prototype
Step 3: Obtain Client Approval	Step 4: Deliver Materials to Client

65. Where does the conversation take place?

(A) At a concert hall
(B) At a museum
(C) At a sports stadium
(D) At a movie theater

66. Look at the graphic. Why is the woman's ticket discounted?

(A) It is a Monday.
(B) It is after 5 P.M.
(C) She is a student.
(D) She is a member.

67. What will the woman most likely do next?

(A) Select a meeting time
(B) Eat at a café
(C) Go on a tour
(D) Attend a lecture

68. What is the main topic of the conversation?

(A) Training materials
(B) Banking hours
(C) Job descriptions
(D) Customer complaints

69. Look at the graphic. When will the speakers need to make a payment?

(A) After Step 1
(B) After Step 2
(C) After Step 3
(D) After Step 4

70. What does the woman say she has been busy doing?

(A) Interviewing candidates
(B) Moving her office
(C) Renovating a house
(D) Finalizing a sale

PART 4

Directions: You will hear some talks given by a single speaker. You will be asked to answer three questions about what the speaker says in each talk. Select the best response to each question and mark the letter (A), (B), (C), or (D) on your answer sheet. The talks will not be printed in your test book and will be spoken only one time.

71. Which department does the speaker work in?

(A) Sales
(B) Human Resources
(C) Maintenance
(D) Technical Support

72. According to the speaker, what will begin today?

(A) Some salary increases
(B) Some building repairs
(C) A landscaping improvement
(D) A departmental audit

73. What does the speaker say will be available to employees?

(A) A shuttle ride
(B) Some meal vouchers
(C) Bottled water
(D) A mentoring program

74. Where is the talk taking place?

(A) At a talent agency
(B) At a history museum
(C) At a flight school
(D) At a movie theater

75. What does the speaker emphasize about a business?

(A) It has a long history.
(B) It is easy to find.
(C) It is reasonably priced.
(D) It has extended hours.

76. What will the listeners do next?

(A) Get on an airplane
(B) Have some refreshments
(C) Purchase a ticket
(D) Watch a film

77. What position is the listener interviewing for?

(A) A travel agent
(B) A journalist
(C) A restaurant chef
(D) A farm manager

78. What does the speaker say he wants to hear about?

(A) A menu selection
(B) A reservation system
(C) A gardening technique
(D) An advertising plan

79. What does the speaker say he will do after the interview?

(A) Introduce a colleague
(B) Contact a reference
(C) Sample some products
(D) Give a tour

80. What is the report mainly about?

(A) A local election
(B) A city festival
(C) A construction project
(D) A sports competition

81. According to the speaker, what can the listeners find on a Web site?

(A) A schedule of events
(B) An updated road map
(C) Tourist attractions
(D) Voting locations

82. What does the speaker mean when she says, "there are several bus lines"?

(A) She rides the bus to work every day.
(B) The bus service is very confusing.
(C) The city buses have caused some traffic problems.
(D) People should take the bus to an event.

GO ON TO THE NEXT PAGE

83. What is the topic of the seminar?

(A) Finance basics
(B) Marketing strategies
(C) Manufacturing processes
(D) Hiring procedures

84. What does the speaker say is available on a Web site?

(A) An electronic book
(B) Different payment options
(C) Free legal advice
(D) Printable certificates

85. What does the speaker ask the listeners to do next?

(A) Introduce themselves
(B) Hand in some paperwork
(C) Read a short paragraph
(D) Listen to some examples

86. Who is the telephone message for?

(A) A dietician
(B) A caterer
(C) A truck driver
(D) A store owner

87. What does the speaker mean when she says, "do you carry local fruit"?

(A) She cannot find the products she is looking for.
(B) She wants the listener to give her some advice.
(C) She wants the listener to sell her products.
(D) She is worried about a shipment.

88. What does the speaker say she can do tomorrow?

(A) Make a phone call
(B) Provide samples
(C) Send an invoice
(D) Visit a clinic

89. Where do the listeners most likely work?

(A) At an event planning company
(B) At an appliance store
(C) At a fitness center
(D) At a hotel

90. What will the listeners learn to use?

(A) Reservation software
(B) A voice-controlled speaker
(C) A video game
(D) A security system

91. What benefit of the product does the speaker mention?

(A) Lower operating costs
(B) Improved customer service
(C) Easier maintenance
(D) Increased employee satisfaction

92. What is the speaker mainly discussing?

(A) A department merger
(B) A project plan
(C) A staffing change
(D) A trade show presentation

93. What are the listeners asked to sign?

(A) A greeting card
(B) A participant list
(C) A group photograph
(D) A registration form

94. Why does the speaker say, "he does have fourteen years of experience"?

(A) To express surprise
(B) To disagree with a suggestion
(C) To correct a misunderstanding
(D) To offer reassurance

International Week Specials

Monday
Korean Barbecue

Tuesday
Italian Pasta

Wednesday
Indian Curry

Thursday
Mexican Tacos

95. Where is the announcement most likely being made?

(A) In an amusement park
(B) In a supermarket
(C) In a restaurant
(D) In an airport lounge

96. Look at the graphic. What is offered today?

(A) Barbecue
(B) Pasta
(C) Curry
(D) Tacos

97. What is provided with a purchase?

(A) Beverages
(B) Serving utensils
(C) Discount coupons
(D) Recipes

Landscapers Showcase Schedule

Presentation	Time
Dealing with Extreme Weather	8:00 A.M.
How to Create a Vertical Garden	9:00 A.M.
New Methods of Pest Control	10:00 A.M.
Urban Landscapes	11:00 A.M.

98. What does the speaker remind the listeners to do?

(A) Pay a registration fee
(B) Pick up conference materials
(C) Visit a vendor's booth
(D) Make a lunch selection

99. Look at the graphic. Which presentation has been canceled?

(A) Dealing with Extreme Weather
(B) How to Create a Vertical Garden
(C) New Methods of Pest Control
(D) Urban Landscapes

100. Who is Rajesh Patel?

(A) A conference organizer
(B) A corporate sponsor
(C) A local caterer
(D) A building inspector

TEST 4

This is the end of the Listening test.

토익˚ 정기시험
기출문제집

LC

기출 TEST

05

LISTENING TEST

In the Listening test, you will be asked to demonstrate how well you understand spoken English. The entire Listening test will last approximately 45 minutes. There are four parts, and directions are given for each part. You must mark your answers on the separate answer sheet. Do not write your answers in your test book.

PART 1

Directions: For each question in this part, you will hear four statements about a picture in your test book. When you hear the statements, you must select the one statement that best describes what you see in the picture. Then find the number of the question on your answer sheet and mark your answer. The statements will not be printed in your test book and will be spoken only one time.

Statement (C), "They're sitting at a table," is the best description of the picture, so you should select answer (C) and mark it on your answer sheet.

1.

2.

GO ON TO THE NEXT PAGE

3.

4.

5.

6.

GO ON TO THE NEXT PAGE ➡

PART 2

Directions: You will hear a question or statement and three responses spoken in English. They will not be printed in your test book and will be spoken only one time. Select the best response to the question or statement and mark the letter (A), (B), or (C) on your answer sheet.

7. Mark your answer on your answer sheet.

8. Mark your answer on your answer sheet.

9. Mark your answer on your answer sheet.

10. Mark your answer on your answer sheet.

11. Mark your answer on your answer sheet.

12. Mark your answer on your answer sheet.

13. Mark your answer on your answer sheet.

14. Mark your answer on your answer sheet.

15. Mark your answer on your answer sheet.

16. Mark your answer on your answer sheet.

17. Mark your answer on your answer sheet.

18. Mark your answer on your answer sheet.

19. Mark your answer on your answer sheet.

20. Mark your answer on your answer sheet.

21. Mark your answer on your answer sheet.

22. Mark your answer on your answer sheet.

23. Mark your answer on your answer sheet.

24. Mark your answer on your answer sheet.

25. Mark your answer on your answer sheet.

26. Mark your answer on your answer sheet.

27. Mark your answer on your answer sheet.

28. Mark your answer on your answer sheet.

29. Mark your answer on your answer sheet.

30. Mark your answer on your answer sheet.

31. Mark your answer on your answer sheet.

Directions: You will hear some conversations between two or more people. You will be asked to answer three questions about what the speakers say in each conversation. Select the best response to each question and mark the letter (A), (B), (C), or (D) on your answer sheet. The conversations will not be printed in your test book and will be spoken only one time.

32. Who most likely is the woman?

(A) A store cashier
(B) A tour guide
(C) A restaurant server
(D) A truck driver

33. What does the man ask the woman about?

(A) Membership rewards
(B) A delivery service
(C) An online payment system
(D) New business hours

34. What will the woman do next?

(A) Call a supervisor
(B) Process a refund
(C) Give some directions
(D) Look for a price list

35. Where are the speakers?

(A) At a park
(B) At a museum
(C) At a bus station
(D) At a concert hall

36. What does the man suggest that the woman do?

(A) Buy a souvenir
(B) Wait outside
(C) Make a reservation
(D) Download a mobile app

37. What does the man give to the woman?

(A) A receipt
(B) A coupon
(C) A map
(D) A postcard

38. Where is the conversation taking place?

(A) At a radio station
(B) At a public library
(C) At a publishing company
(D) At an import-export firm

39. What is the purpose of the man's visit?

(A) To propose an advertising plan
(B) To make a repair
(C) To interview for a job
(D) To lead a training session

40. What does the man say he is willing to do?

(A) Lower a fee
(B) Upgrade some software
(C) Rush an order
(D) Travel internationally

41. Where do the speakers most likely work?

(A) At an employment agency
(B) At a rental car office
(C) At a hospital
(D) At a hotel

42. What does the woman give the man?

(A) Some flight information
(B) Some meal vouchers
(C) A map of local attractions
(D) A parking permit

43. Why does the woman say, "We have enough people to cover your shifts"?

(A) To refuse an offer
(B) To approve a request
(C) To emphasize the importance of an assignment
(D) To complain that an employee is late

GO ON TO THE NEXT PAGE

44. What event are the speakers preparing for?

(A) A trade show
(B) A factory visit
(C) A grand opening
(D) A product launch

45. Why has the woman delayed a task?

(A) There was a data-entry mistake.
(B) A registration form was missing.
(C) Ticket prices are expensive.
(D) Attendance rates are too low.

46. What does the woman say she will do?

(A) Review a presentation
(B) Look at a Web site
(C) Print an itinerary
(D) Pick up a client

47. Why was the man told to arrive early to the appointment?

(A) To make a payment
(B) To get an X-ray
(C) To pick up a prescription
(D) To complete some paperwork

48. What does the man say about his previous doctor?

(A) She recently retired.
(B) She is highly rated by patients.
(C) She has moved out of the area.
(D) She specialized in sports medicine.

49. What is the reason for the appointment?

(A) Allergies
(B) Headaches
(C) A cough
(D) An injury

50. Which field does the man most likely work in?

(A) Engineering
(B) Transportation
(C) Manufacturing
(D) Construction

51. What does the man say has arrived?

(A) A design sketch
(B) A contract
(C) A shipment
(D) Some cleaning products

52. What does the woman mean when she says, "You have the key to the storage unit, right"?

(A) She wants a door to remain locked.
(B) She wants to inspect a facility.
(C) She wants the man to put some supplies away.
(D) She wants to confirm that only one key exists.

53. Who most likely is the man?

(A) A fashion designer
(B) A software developer
(C) A marketing consultant
(D) A personnel manager

54. According to the woman, what has caused a problem?

(A) A missed deadline
(B) A shortage of staff members
(C) An increase in customers
(D) A mistake in some promotional materials

55. What does the man say he will do by the end of the day?

(A) Send a department memo
(B) Review some job applications
(C) Research some competitors
(D) Provide a time estimate

56. What type of business are the speakers discussing?

(A) A café
(B) A clothing store
(C) A medical clinic
(D) A fitness center

57. What do the speakers like about the business?

(A) It is located near their workplace.
(B) It has a customer loyalty program.
(C) It has friendly staff members.
(D) It is open every day.

58. What is the business offering this month?

(A) Expedited shipping
(B) Parking validation
(C) Discounted merchandise
(D) Online consultations

59. What does one of the men say they are accustomed to?

(A) Preparing estimates
(B) Working in various weather conditions
(C) Last-minute schedule changes
(D) Long commutes to job sites

60. Why are the men visiting the factory?

(A) To inspect some pipes
(B) To sign a business agreement
(C) To measure energy usage
(D) To install some machinery

61. What does one of the men warn the woman about?

(A) Some materials may not be available.
(B) Some prices may increase.
(C) A business may relocate.
(D) A building may have to be closed temporarily.

Today's Specials

Food	Price	Free Soft Drink
Candy	$3.00	Small
Chips	$4.00	Medium
Hot dog	$5.50	Large
Popcorn	$7.00	Super

62. Where are the speakers?

(A) At a sports arena
(B) At a restaurant
(C) At a movie theater
(D) At a community picnic

63. Look at the graphic. What size drink will the man receive?

(A) Small
(B) Medium
(C) Large
(D) Super

64. How will the man pay?

(A) With a credit card
(B) With a gift certificate
(C) With a coupon
(D) With cash

GO ON TO THE NEXT PAGE

Itinerary

Monday—arrival at airport, dinner

Tuesday—factory tour, art museum

Wednesday—executive meeting, basketball game

Thursday—morning departure

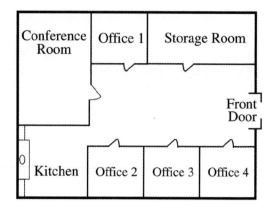

65. Why are the speakers changing the itinerary?

(A) A client has made a request.
(B) A venue is too small.
(C) A ticket price is too high.
(D) A presenter has been delayed.

66. What activity will the speakers add to the itinerary?

(A) A theater performance
(B) A hiking trip
(C) A shopping trip
(D) A garden show

67. Look at the graphic. On which day will an activity be replaced?

(A) Monday
(B) Tuesday
(C) Wednesday
(D) Thursday

68. Why is the man familiar with the office?

(A) He used to work there.
(B) He was there for an interview.
(C) He was e-mailed a floor plan.
(D) He was given a tour by a friend.

69. Look at the graphic. Which office does the woman recommend?

(A) Office 1
(B) Office 2
(C) Office 3
(D) Office 4

70. What will the woman explain later?

(A) How to access a network
(B) How to request a printer
(C) How to file some documents
(D) How to obtain a parking pass

Directions: You will hear some talks given by a single speaker. You will be asked to answer three questions about what the speaker says in each talk. Select the best response to each question and mark the letter (A), (B), (C), or (D) on your answer sheet. The talks will not be printed in your test book and will be spoken only one time.

71. Where does the talk take place?

    (A) At a supermarket
    (B) At a bakery
    (C) At a farm
    (D) At a restaurant

72. According to the speaker, what is a new task this summer?

    (A) Organizing a festival
    (B) Coordinating with a charity
    (C) Managing a food cart
    (D) Leading cooking classes

73. What can the listeners receive from Anya?

    (A) A map of the facility
    (B) A list of open positions
    (C) A reimbursement form
    (D) A letter of recommendation

74. What is the workshop about?

    (A) Searching a database
    (B) Improving writing skills
    (C) Editing digital photographs
    (D) Creating a Web page

75. According to the speaker, what do the listeners need to access a computer?

    (A) A driver's license
    (B) A receipt
    (C) A credit card
    (D) A library card

76. Why does the speaker say, "I'm at the information desk every evening"?

    (A) To provide a correction
    (B) To reject an invitation
    (C) To offer assistance
    (D) To request a change

77. Why is the speaker calling?

    (A) To ask how to fill out an application
    (B) To inquire about a delivery date
    (C) To report a problem with a product
    (D) To revise a billing address

78. What does the speaker say she is going to do next week?

    (A) Start a new job
    (B) Present at a conference
    (C) Have a dental examination
    (D) Take a trip

79. What does the speaker want the listener to do?

    (A) Provide an extended warranty
    (B) Return a phone call
    (C) Send a new catalog
    (D) Deliver a free sample

80. Why does the speaker congratulate the listener?

    (A) She started a business.
    (B) She won an award.
    (C) She finalized a contract.
    (D) She gave a presentation.

81. What does the speaker say about a newspaper advertisement?

    (A) It will be finished shortly.
    (B) It has increased business.
    (C) It needs to be modified.
    (D) It is well under budget.

82. What does the speaker mean when he says, "many companies are moving to suburban areas just outside the city"?

    (A) He will be moving to another city.
    (B) He is worried about a new policy.
    (C) Pollution in surrounding areas will probably increase.
    (D) A different sales strategy should be considered.

TEST 5

GO ON TO THE NEXT PAGE

83. Where do the listeners most likely work?

(A) At a delivery company
(B) At a repair shop
(C) At an appliance store
(D) At a restaurant

84. What does the speaker say will happen tomorrow?

(A) The hours of operation will be extended.
(B) Some new equipment will be installed.
(C) An anniversary party will be held.
(D) A building inspection will take place.

85. What are the listeners asked to do?

(A) Study an updated menu
(B) Wear a specific uniform
(C) Read a set of instructions
(D) Sign up for extra work shifts

86. What is the main topic of the course?

(A) Computer programming
(B) Factory management
(C) Automotive repair
(D) Mobile phone sales

87. According to the speaker, how is this year's course different from last year's?

(A) It will be shorter.
(B) It will be more expensive.
(C) It will be offered in the evening.
(D) It will be taught by a new instructor.

88. What will the speaker do next?

(A) Distribute a course catalog
(B) Process admissions payments
(C) Assign student ID numbers
(D) Discuss the enrollment process

89. What does the speaker mean when he says, "we have a lot of material to cover today"?

(A) He is upset about an assignment.
(B) He wants to begin immediately.
(C) He is too busy to attend a meeting.
(D) He needs assistance with a presentation.

90. What is the topic of the workshop?

(A) Effective communication skills
(B) Managing department finances
(C) Improving productivity
(D) Choosing job applicants

91. What are the listeners instructed to do?

(A) Submit a résumé
(B) Log in to a database
(C) Show identification
(D) Work with a partner

92. Who most likely is the speaker?

(A) An accountant
(B) An attorney
(C) A real estate agent
(D) A building contractor

93. According to the speaker, what is the problem?

(A) An estimate is higher than expected.
(B) Some work is behind schedule.
(C) A staff member is away.
(D) Some materials are unavailable.

94. What solution does the speaker suggest?

(A) Hiring a smaller team
(B) Paying with a credit card
(C) Completing a project in stages
(D) Buying a different property

Telephone Directory	
Extension	Employee
35	Robert Sanchez
78	Regina Dover
14	Jim Strickland
90	Lucy Cho

95. Where does the speaker most likely work?

(A) At a bank
(B) At a fitness center
(C) At a medical office
(D) At an electronics store

96. Look at the graphic. Who can answer questions about billing?

(A) Robert Sanchez
(B) Regina Dover
(C) Jim Strickland
(D) Lucy Cho

97. What are the listeners asked to do on a Web site?

(A) Fill out a membership form
(B) Learn about an updated policy
(C) Read some nutrition tips
(D) Submit employee biographies

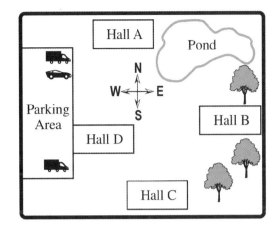

98. Why did employees dislike a proposal?

(A) Construction noise would be disruptive.
(B) A parking fee would increase.
(C) A location would be inconvenient.
(D) Outdoor seating space would be limited.

99. Look at the graphic. Which hall will have a new wing added?

(A) Hall A
(B) Hall B
(C) Hall C
(D) Hall D

100. What will the speaker discuss next?

(A) A timeline
(B) A budget
(C) An upcoming celebration
(D) A volunteer project

This is the end of the Listening test.

토익 정기시험
기출문제집

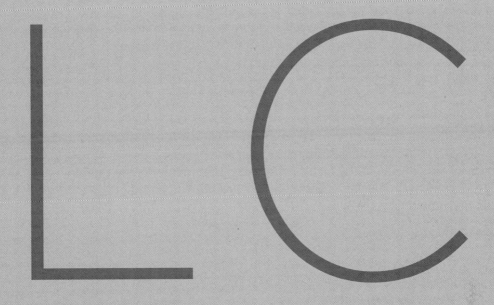

LC

기출 TEST

06

LISTENING TEST

In the Listening test, you will be asked to demonstrate how well you understand spoken English. The entire Listening test will last approximately 45 minutes. There are four parts, and directions are given for each part. You must mark your answers on the separate answer sheet. Do not write your answers in your test book.

PART 1

Directions: For each question in this part, you will hear four statements about a picture in your test book. When you hear the statements, you must select the one statement that best describes what you see in the picture. Then find the number of the question on your answer sheet and mark your answer. The statements will not be printed in your test book and will be spoken only one time.

Statement (C), "They're sitting at a table," is the best description of the picture, so you should select answer (C) and mark it on your answer sheet.

1.

2.

GO ON TO THE NEXT PAGE ➤

3.

4.

5.

6.

GO ON TO THE NEXT PAGE ➤

PART 2

Directions: You will hear a question or statement and three responses spoken in English. They will not be printed in your test book and will be spoken only one time. Select the best response to the question or statement and mark the letter (A), (B), or (C) on your answer sheet.

7. Mark your answer on your answer sheet.

8. Mark your answer on your answer sheet.

9. Mark your answer on your answer sheet.

10. Mark your answer on your answer sheet.

11. Mark your answer on your answer sheet.

12. Mark your answer on your answer sheet.

13. Mark your answer on your answer sheet.

14. Mark your answer on your answer sheet.

15. Mark your answer on your answer sheet.

16. Mark your answer on your answer sheet.

17. Mark your answer on your answer sheet.

18. Mark your answer on your answer sheet.

19. Mark your answer on your answer sheet.

20. Mark your answer on your answer sheet.

21. Mark your answer on your answer sheet.

22. Mark your answer on your answer sheet.

23. Mark your answer on your answer sheet.

24. Mark your answer on your answer sheet.

25. Mark your answer on your answer sheet.

26. Mark your answer on your answer sheet.

27. Mark your answer on your answer sheet.

28. Mark your answer on your answer sheet.

29. Mark your answer on your answer sheet.

30. Mark your answer on your answer sheet.

31. Mark your answer on your answer sheet.

PART 3

Directions: You will hear some conversations between two or more people. You will be asked to answer three questions about what the speakers say in each conversation. Select the best response to each question and mark the letter (A), (B), (C), or (D) on your answer sheet. The conversations will not be printed in your test book and will be spoken only one time.

32. What is the woman trying to do?

(A) Buy a computer
(B) Reserve a flight
(C) Mail a package
(D) Pick up a vehicle

33. What did the woman forget to bring?

(A) A credit card
(B) A confirmation number
(C) Some coupons
(D) Some identification

34. What does the man say he will do?

(A) Search a database
(B) Explain a contract
(C) Talk to a manager
(D) Prepare a shipment

35. Why did the man go to Amy's office?

(A) To request some time off
(B) To demonstrate a product
(C) To drop off some paperwork
(D) To schedule an appointment

36. Why is Amy unavailable?

(A) She is preparing to travel.
(B) She is speaking with a client.
(C) She is attending a seminar.
(D) She is working on a report.

37. What will the man most likely do next?

(A) Meet a colleague for lunch
(B) Conduct a training session
(C) Clean a meeting room
(D) Print some instructions

38. Why is the woman calling?

(A) To update an address
(B) To make a complaint
(C) To renew a subscription
(D) To inquire about employment

39. Why does the man apologize?

(A) A discount does not apply.
(B) A service agreement has ended.
(C) A business has closed.
(D) A security procedure has changed.

40. What does the man say he will do?

(A) Change a delivery time
(B) Send a document
(C) Speak with a supervisor
(D) Provide a phone number

41. Where do the speakers most likely work?

(A) At a manufacturing company
(B) At a grocery store
(C) At an employment agency
(D) At a shipping service

42. According to the men, what is causing a problem?

(A) Some workers have called in sick.
(B) A vehicle has broken down.
(C) A machine is operating slowly.
(D) The boxes are the wrong size.

43. What does the woman suggest?

(A) Checking a warranty
(B) Postponing an inspection
(C) Purchasing a different product
(D) Scheduling a repair

GO ON TO THE NEXT PAGE

44. What are the speakers discussing?

(A) A new product
(B) A company merger
(C) Cost estimates
(D) Survey results

45. According to the man, what is the main problem?

(A) His team is unable to complete a project on time.
(B) Some employees did not receive a salary increase.
(C) There is too much noise in the office.
(D) There are not enough parking spaces.

46. What does the woman suggest doing?

(A) Reminding people about a company policy
(B) Hiring some temporary staff
(C) Moving to a different building
(D) Speaking to the management team

47. What is the woman calling about?

(A) Processing a payment
(B) Printing invitations
(C) Hiring extra help
(D) Filling an order

48. What does the man imply when he says, "the request came directly from the client"?

(A) Some contact information is incorrect.
(B) A change is not possible.
(C) A worker is highly qualified.
(D) A fee has been discussed.

49. What does the woman say she will do?

(A) Revise a bill
(B) Set up a meeting
(C) Contact some businesses
(D) Pack some merchandise

50. What did the woman win a prize for?

(A) Having the highest sales numbers
(B) Providing excellent customer service
(C) Working at the company for ten years
(D) Reducing costs on a project

51. What will the woman do this weekend?

(A) Visit a branch office
(B) Attend a conference
(C) Join a fitness club
(D) Go on a vacation

52. What does the woman say she will do with the prize?

(A) Display it in her office
(B) Exchange it at the store
(C) Offer it to someone else
(D) Use it at a later date

53. Where does the conversation most likely take place?

(A) In a train station
(B) In a hotel
(C) In a theater
(D) In a computer store

54. Why does the man say, "This is my first visit here"?

(A) To explain his concern
(B) To provide an excuse
(C) To ask for permission
(D) To request a recommendation

55. Why does the woman recommend making a purchase on the Internet?

(A) More products are available.
(B) It is not necessary to wait in line.
(C) The price is reduced.
(D) Shipping is free.

56. Which industry do the speakers most likely work in?

(A) Home construction
(B) Finance
(C) Web design
(D) Health care

57. What does the man recommend?

(A) Hiring an accountant
(B) Changing operating hours
(C) Purchasing office supplies
(D) Revising a timeline

58. What does the woman say she will do?

(A) Pick up an application
(B) Submit an invoice
(C) Schedule a workshop
(D) Make an appointment

59. Why is the woman at Regal Advertising?

(A) For a photography session
(B) For a client consultation
(C) For a job interview
(D) For a building opening

60. What does the woman say is her specialty?

(A) Researching international laws
(B) Creating designs for billboards
(C) Building a strong customer base
(D) Finding cost-efficient business solutions

61. What does the woman say she appreciates about Regal?

(A) The company creates unique designs.
(B) The company has offices overseas.
(C) The company is dedicated to research.
(D) The company values its employees.

Destination	Departure Time	Status
Los Angeles	10:00	Delayed– one hour
San Antonio	10:30	On time
San Jose	11:00	On time
Las Vegas	11:30	Delayed– 30 minutes

62. What problem does the woman report?

(A) She forgot to bring a laptop.
(B) She is running late.
(C) A flight was overbooked.
(D) A guest speaker canceled.

63. Look at the graphic. Where are the speakers going?

(A) To Los Angeles
(B) To San Antonio
(C) To San Jose
(D) To Las Vegas

64. What does the woman ask the man to do?

(A) Postpone an event
(B) Borrow some equipment
(C) File a complaint
(D) Make a phone call

GO ON TO THE NEXT PAGE

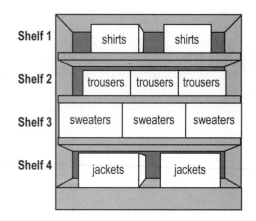

Shelf 1 — shirts shirts
Shelf 2 — trousers trousers trousers
Shelf 3 — sweaters sweaters sweaters
Shelf 4 — jackets jackets

Business Plan

Part 1 ......Company Overview

Part 2 ......Services

Part 3 ......Industry Analysis

Part 4 ......Advertising

Part 5 ......Budget

65. What problem does the woman mention?

(A) Some labels are incorrect.
(B) An item is unpopular.
(C) A shipment is delayed.
(D) More storage space is needed.

66. Look at the graphic. Which shelf will the man work on today?

(A) Shelf 1
(B) Shelf 2
(C) Shelf 3
(D) Shelf 4

67. What does the woman tell the man to do?

(A) Sign for a delivery
(B) Put price tags on some items
(C) Contact a different supplier
(D) Move a display table

68. What kind of business does the man want to start?

(A) A shop
(B) A restaurant
(C) A bank
(D) A farm

69. What does the man say he learned from his previous business?

(A) How to apply for an operating permit
(B) How to negotiate a vendor contract
(C) How to make attractive advertisements
(D) How to identify potential customers

70. Look at the graphic. Which part of the business plan does the woman suggest revising?

(A) Part 2
(B) Part 3
(C) Part 4
(D) Part 5

Directions: You will hear some talks given by a single speaker. You will be asked to answer three questions about what the speaker says in each talk. Select the best response to each question and mark the letter (A), (B), (C), or (D) on your answer sheet. The talks will not be printed in your test book and will be spoken only one time.

71. What industry does the speaker most likely work in?

(A) Information Technology
(B) Shipping and Receiving
(C) Advertising
(D) Manufacturing

72. What is the speaker mainly talking about?

(A) A budget proposal
(B) Product designs
(C) A project delay
(D) Sample photos

73. What are the listeners asked to do?

(A) Review a schedule
(B) Work overtime
(C) Suggest some ideas
(D) Prepare a presentation

74. What is the main purpose of the message?

(A) To complain about parking
(B) To confirm a move-in date
(C) To discuss a rent increase
(D) To report a broken appliance

75. What does the speaker say he did yesterday?

(A) He started a new job.
(B) He talked to his neighbors.
(C) He helped a friend move.
(D) He went to a party.

76. What does the speaker plan to do tomorrow?

(A) Attend a music concert
(B) Borrow a vehicle
(C) Pay a late bill
(D) Stop by an office

77. Where do the listeners probably work?

(A) At an accounting firm
(B) At a software company
(C) At a travel agency
(D) At a shipping warehouse

78. What does the speaker imply when she says, "Now, there's a box in the staff room"?

(A) Some materials have been relocated.
(B) A shipment is urgent.
(C) A problem has been solved.
(D) A task was not completed.

79. What will the speaker do on Fridays?

(A) Meet with clients
(B) Make deliveries
(C) Summarize feedback
(D) Inspect facilities

80. What type of business recorded the message?

(A) A construction company
(B) A law firm
(C) An electronics manufacturer
(D) An insurance agency

81. What does the speaker say about the office?

(A) It has moved to a different location.
(B) Its business hours have changed.
(C) It is closed for a holiday.
(D) It is being renovated.

82. What are the listeners instructed to do?

(A) Send an e-mail
(B) Visit a Web site
(C) Call at a later time
(D) Fill out a form

TEST 6

83. What is the broadcast mainly about?

(A) Projected employment figures
(B) An international fashion conference
(C) An advertising campaign
(D) The relocation of a business

84. According to the speaker, who is Sharon Rockford?

(A) An architect
(B) A fashion designer
(C) A company president
(D) A magazine editor

85. What is Broadchurch Fashions planning to do next spring?

(A) Introduce a woman's clothing line
(B) Hire a celebrity spokesperson
(C) Start an online business
(D) Sponsor a charitable event

86. What kind of equipment has just been installed?

(A) Shredders
(B) Projectors
(C) Computers
(D) Printers

87. What product feature does the speaker emphasize?

(A) It is energy efficient.
(B) It is durable.
(C) It is secure.
(D) It is inexpensive.

88. Why does the speaker say, "but they're generally very busy"?

(A) To complain about a difficult work schedule
(B) To offer to repair some equipment
(C) To encourage the listeners to be patient
(D) To suggest hiring more staff

89. Where does the speaker most likely work?

(A) At a driving school
(B) At an automobile dealership
(C) At a manufacturing plant
(D) At a delivery service

90. What did the survey gather information about?

(A) Safety practices
(B) Employee engagement
(C) Interest in new merchandise
(D) Customer satisfaction

91. What incentive did the company provide for returning the survey?

(A) A promotional T-shirt
(B) A product upgrade
(C) A free car wash
(D) A gift card

92. Who most likely are the listeners?

(A) Sales representatives
(B) Property managers
(C) Electrical engineers
(D) Maintenance workers

93. What does the speaker imply when she says, "most people have a limited understanding of the topic"?

(A) A product must be redesigned.
(B) A topic should be explained clearly.
(C) A mistake could not be avoided.
(D) A task can only be done by professionals.

94. According to the woman, what is the listeners' goal?

(A) To meet a quota
(B) To lower expenses
(C) To recruit more employees
(D) To collaborate more effectively

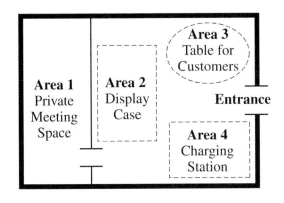

MEMBERSHIP FORM

$40 Student _____	$150 Family _____
$80 Individual _____	$500 Business _____

Name: _____

Credit Card Number: _____

Expiration Date: _____ / _____

95. Who most likely is the speaker?

(A) An architect
(B) A store supervisor
(C) An event organizer
(D) An electrician

96. What does the speaker say about mobile phones?

(A) They have been discounted recently.
(B) They will be centrally located.
(C) They can be updated quickly.
(D) They must be turned off now.

97. Look at the graphic. Which area was added?

(A) Area 1
(B) Area 2
(C) Area 3
(D) Area 4

98. Where does the speaker most likely work?

(A) At a library
(B) At a fitness center
(C) At a zoo
(D) At a museum

99. What does the speaker thank the listeners for?

(A) Signing up for membership
(B) Leading group tours
(C) Agreeing to help with a project
(D) Registering for a newsletter

100. Look at the graphic. Which amount has changed this year?

(A) $40
(B) $80
(C) $150
(D) $500

TEST 6

This is the end of the Listening test.

토익˚ 정기시험
기출문제집

LC

기출 TEST

07

LISTENING TEST

In the Listening test, you will be asked to demonstrate how well you understand spoken English. The entire Listening test will last approximately 45 minutes. There are four parts, and directions are given for each part. You must mark your answers on the separate answer sheet. Do not write your answers in your test book.

PART 1

Directions: For each question in this part, you will hear four statements about a picture in your test book. When you hear the statements, you must select the one statement that best describes what you see in the picture. Then find the number of the question on your answer sheet and mark your answer. The statements will not be printed in your test book and will be spoken only one time.

Statement (C), "They're sitting at a table," is the best description of the picture, so you should select answer (C) and mark it on your answer sheet.

1.

2.

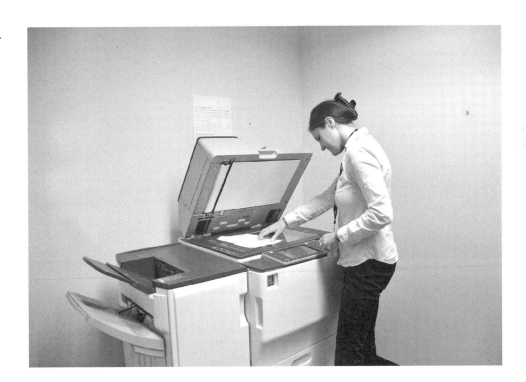

GO ON TO THE NEXT PAGE

3.

4.

5.

6.

GO ON TO THE NEXT PAGE

PART 2

Directions: You will hear a question or statement and three responses spoken in English. They will not be printed in your test book and will be spoken only one time. Select the best response to the question or statement and mark the letter (A), (B), or (C) on your answer sheet.

7. Mark your answer on your answer sheet.

8. Mark your answer on your answer sheet.

9. Mark your answer on your answer sheet.

10. Mark your answer on your answer sheet.

11. Mark your answer on your answer sheet.

12. Mark your answer on your answer sheet.

13. Mark your answer on your answer sheet.

14. Mark your answer on your answer sheet.

15. Mark your answer on your answer sheet.

16. Mark your answer on your answer sheet.

17. Mark your answer on your answer sheet.

18. Mark your answer on your answer sheet.

19. Mark your answer on your answer sheet.

20. Mark your answer on your answer sheet.

21. Mark your answer on your answer sheet.

22. Mark your answer on your answer sheet.

23. Mark your answer on your answer sheet.

24. Mark your answer on your answer sheet.

25. Mark your answer on your answer sheet.

26. Mark your answer on your answer sheet.

27. Mark your answer on your answer sheet.

28. Mark your answer on your answer sheet.

29. Mark your answer on your answer sheet.

30. Mark your answer on your answer sheet.

31. Mark your answer on your answer sheet.

Directions: You will hear some conversations between two or more people. You will be asked to answer three questions about what the speakers say in each conversation. Select the best response to each question and mark the letter (A), (B), (C), or (D) on your answer sheet. The conversations will not be printed in your test book and will be spoken only one time.

32. Where are the speakers?

(A) At a hotel
(B) At a museum
(C) At a clothing store
(D) At a movie theater

33. What problem does the woman have?

(A) She lost her gloves.
(B) She cannot find her tour group.
(C) She forgot her wallet.
(D) She needs directions.

34. What does the man ask for?

(A) A phone number
(B) A photo ID card
(C) A receipt
(D) A confirmation code

35. Where do the speakers work?

(A) At a restaurant
(B) At a national park
(C) At an outdoor market
(D) At a grocery store

36. Who is Julia?

(A) A trainee
(B) An investor
(C) A customer
(D) A supervisor

37. What will Julia most likely do next?

(A) Go on a hike
(B) Receive a payment
(C) Revise an itinerary
(D) Get a uniform

38. What is the man planning for next month?

(A) A birthday dinner
(B) An awards banquet
(C) A retirement party
(D) An office relocation

39. What does the woman say she will do?

(A) Send a sample menu
(B) Prepare a contract
(C) Change a reservation
(D) Speak to a manager

40. What will the man give to the woman?

(A) A guest list
(B) An e-mail address
(C) A credit card number
(D) An itinerary

41. Where does the conversation take place?

(A) At a fitness center
(B) At a pharmacy
(C) At a travel agency
(D) At a bank

42. What does the woman say she will do next month?

(A) Take a vacation
(B) Start a new job
(C) See a different doctor
(D) Move to a new city

43. Why does Jason talk to Mr. Pruitt?

(A) To ask about a policy
(B) To notify him of a scheduling change
(C) To introduce him to a friend
(D) To request that a machine be repaired

GO ON TO THE NEXT PAGE

44. Who most likely is the woman?

   (A) A computer engineer
   (B) A maintenance worker
   (C) A customer service representative
   (D) A television journalist

45. Why does the woman say, "there was a heavy snowstorm last week"?

   (A) To explain why a delivery was delayed
   (B) To report on a recent power failure
   (C) To approve some employee absences
   (D) To explain why some property is damaged

46. What does the man say he will do soon?

   (A) Travel to another city
   (B) Choose a mobile phone provider
   (C) Post a job announcement
   (D) Begin working from home

---

47. Which industry do the speakers work in?

   (A) Internet technology
   (B) Real estate
   (C) Manufacturing
   (D) Banking

48. What change is the man proposing?

   (A) Taking out a loan
   (B) Finding a different supplier
   (C) Building another factory
   (D) Expanding a sales area

49. What does the woman offer to do?

   (A) Make a pricing decision
   (B) Contact a retail chain
   (C) Record a promotional video
   (D) Revise a database

---

50. What does the woman want to do?

   (A) Verify a contract
   (B) Rent a storage unit
   (C) Dispose of some documents
   (D) Install some machines

51. What is the woman concerned about?

   (A) Whether some containers are secure
   (B) Whether some clients have arrived
   (C) Whether a truck is locked
   (D) Whether a space is available

52. How often does the woman want a service?

   (A) Daily
   (B) Weekly
   (C) Monthly
   (D) Yearly

---

53. What is the woman calling about?

   (A) A missing reservation
   (B) A messy room
   (C) Broken equipment
   (D) Transportation delays

54. What does the woman imply when she says, "I do have clients coming in at eleven o'clock"?

   (A) She needs a task to be completed quickly.
   (B) She is agreeing to postpone a conference.
   (C) She realizes her calendar is incorrect.
   (D) She is pleased about a business deal.

55. What does the man say he will do?

   (A) Provide a refund
   (B) Prepare a receipt
   (C) Call an employee
   (D) Review a project timeline

---

56. What type of event will the speakers attend?

(A) A professional seminar
(B) A board meeting
(C) A safety training
(D) An awards ceremony

57. What does the man ask about?

(A) A certification requirement
(B) A reimbursement process
(C) A presentation schedule
(D) A building location

58. What does the woman recommend the man do?

(A) Speak with his supervisor
(B) Update his résumé
(C) E-mail an event planner
(D) Watch a video tutorial

59. Where do the speakers work?

(A) At a newspaper company
(B) At a city government office
(C) At a train station
(D) At a construction firm

60. What are the speakers mainly discussing?

(A) A bicycle sale
(B) A bicycle race
(C) A bicycle-safety class
(D) A bicycle-sharing program

61. What does the woman suggest doing later today?

(A) Celebrating an accomplishment
(B) Negotiating a business deal
(C) Interviewing some participants
(D) Holding a press conference

Minor League Soccer
Regular Season Results

Team	Games Won
Gold Town	10
Lakeview	9
Dover	8
Santa Rosa	6

62. Look at the graphic. Which team do the speakers support?

(A) Gold Town
(B) Lakeview
(C) Dover
(D) Santa Rosa

63. What does the man offer to do?

(A) Join a sports team
(B) Record a sporting event
(C) Print some bus maps
(D) Give some colleagues a ride

64. What does the woman remind the man about?

(A) A group discount
(B) Extended bus service
(C) An approaching work deadline
(D) The opening of a new sports facility

GO ON TO THE NEXT PAGE

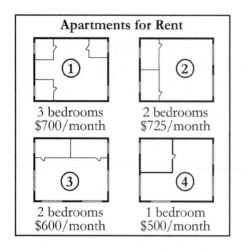

Apartments for Rent

① 3 bedrooms $700/month

② 2 bedrooms $725/month

③ 2 bedrooms $600/month

④ 1 bedroom $500/month

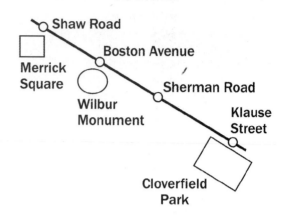

ROUTE 11

Shaw Road
Merrick Square
Boston Avenue
Wilbur Monument
Sherman Road
Klause Street
Cloverfield Park

65. Why does the woman say she is moving to Watertown?

(A) She wants a shorter commute.
(B) She is starting her own business.
(C) Her family lives in the area.
(D) Her company is relocating.

66. Look at the graphic. Which apartment is the woman most interested in?

(A) Apartment 1
(B) Apartment 2
(C) Apartment 3
(D) Apartment 4

67. What will the speakers most likely do next?

(A) Schedule a visit
(B) Finish some designs
(C) Review a lease agreement
(D) Look at some furniture

68. Why does the woman say she is late?

(A) She had a long meeting.
(B) She was having car trouble.
(C) There was a lot of traffic.
(D) A client arrived unexpectedly.

69. What does the woman ask the man to do?

(A) Give her a ride to the office
(B) Meet her at a bus stop
(C) Call an important client
(D) Pick up a bus ticket

70. Look at the graphic. Which bus stop is the woman close to now?

(A) Shaw Road
(B) Boston Avenue
(C) Sherman Road
(D) Klause Street

PART 4

Directions: You will hear some talks given by a single speaker. You will be asked to answer three questions about what the speaker says in each talk. Select the best response to each question and mark the letter (A), (B), (C), or (D) on your answer sheet. The talks will not be printed in your test book and will be spoken only one time.

71. Where is the announcement being made?

    (A) At an electronics store
    (B) At a clothing shop
    (C) At a hardware store
    (D) At a supermarket

72. What service is going to be offered?

    (A) Online ordering
    (B) Gift wrapping
    (C) Rentals
    (D) Repairs

73. Why should the listeners go to the customer service desk?

    (A) To fill out a survey
    (B) To register for discounts
    (C) To pick up a brochure
    (D) To get free samples

74. What is the listener trying to do?

    (A) Meet a film director
    (B) Make a reservation
    (C) Enter a contest
    (D) Apply for a job

75. What does the speaker imply when he says, "a film festival is taking place here that week"?

    (A) He recommends going to an event.
    (B) He cannot fulfill a request.
    (C) A city is becoming more popular.
    (D) There will be a lot of traffic.

76. What did the speaker do for the listener?

    (A) He reviewed an employment application.
    (B) He purchased some event tickets.
    (C) He confirmed a flight itinerary.
    (D) He contacted another branch location.

77. Who most likely are the listeners?

    (A) Sales assistants
    (B) Factory workers
    (C) Hiring managers
    (D) Delivery drivers

78. What does the speaker remind the listeners about?

    (A) Referring to a handbook
    (B) Organizing merchandise
    (C) Filling out a time sheet
    (D) Greeting customers

79. According to the speaker, what might the listeners receive?

    (A) Free products
    (B) Extra vacation days
    (C) A cash bonus
    (D) A gift certificate

80. Where does the speaker work?

    (A) At a fitness center
    (B) At a doctor's office
    (C) At a laboratory
    (D) At a pharmacy

81. Why is the speaker calling?

    (A) To confirm an appointment
    (B) To provide a reference
    (C) To discuss lab results
    (D) To resolve a billing issue

82. What does the speaker say happened last month?

    (A) A building lobby was renovated.
    (B) An office moved to a different floor.
    (C) Some fees increased.
    (D) Some employees were hired.

GO ON TO THE NEXT PAGE

83. What has a government department recently announced?

(A) Job opportunities
(B) Funding decisions
(C) New transportation regulations
(D) Updated construction plans

84. What is being advertised?

(A) A car wash service
(B) A training program
(C) A navigation system
(D) An insurance policy

85. What does the speaker say will happen next week?

(A) A discount offer will end.
(B) A store location will open.
(C) A product will be launched.
(D) A facility will be inspected.

---

86. What type of event is taking place?

(A) A gallery opening
(B) A retirement party
(C) An awards ceremony
(D) A school fund-raiser

87. What happened in June?

(A) A building was purchased.
(B) A marketing campaign began.
(C) Some deadlines were extended.
(D) Some artists were selected.

88. What does the speaker imply when she says, "tourism in the area has doubled"?

(A) A project was successful.
(B) More volunteers are needed.
(C) Renovation work can begin.
(D) It is difficult to find parking.

89. What will Dr. Ray speak about?

(A) Managing financial risk
(B) Communicating with patients
(C) Improving customer service
(D) Preparing for job interviews

90. What is Dr. Ray's current position?

(A) He is the editor of a publication.
(B) He is a professor at a university.
(C) He is the chief surgeon at a hospital.
(D) He is a safety inspector in a laboratory.

91. What will Dr. Ray do after his speech?

(A) Sign some books
(B) Attend a reception
(C) Demonstrate a technique
(D) Evaluate a financial record

---

92. Where does the speaker most likely work?

(A) At a mobile phone manufacturer
(B) At a radio station
(C) At an Internet service provider
(D) At a clothing store

93. What does the speaker mean when he says, "but the phones are still ringing"?

(A) The company continues to receive complaints.
(B) The company needs additional staff.
(C) The company is still taking orders.
(D) The company's advertising was effective.

94. What will the listeners most likely do next?

(A) Promote a business
(B) Revise some résumé
(C) Make a repair
(D) Read a document

Cake Recipes

Vanilla
Vanilla cake mix + Cherry Soda

Chocolate
Chocolate cake mix + Cola

Lemon
Lemon cake mix + Lemon Soda

Strawberry
Strawberry cake mix + Ginger ale

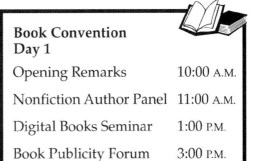

Book Convention Day 1

Opening Remarks	10:00 A.M.
Nonfiction Author Panel	11:00 A.M.
Digital Books Seminar	1:00 P.M.
Book Publicity Forum	3:00 P.M.

95. Who is the intended audience for the broadcast?

(A) Restaurant owners
(B) Home cooks
(C) Food critics
(D) Professional chefs

96. Look at the graphic. Which cake recipe did the speaker change?

(A) Vanilla
(B) Chocolate
(C) Lemon
(D) Strawberry

97. What are the listeners asked to do?

(A) Call the show
(B) Attend a class
(C) Share photographs
(D) Write a review

98. Where is the talk most likely taking place?

(A) At a library
(B) At a bookstore
(C) At a publishing company
(D) At a news agency

99. Look at the graphic. Which session are the listeners required to attend?

(A) Opening Remarks
(B) Nonfiction Author Panel
(C) Digital Books Seminar
(D) Book Publicity Forum

100. What still needs to be confirmed?

(A) The event location
(B) The registration fee
(C) The start time
(D) The catering arrangements

This is the end of the Listening test.

토익® 정기시험
기출문제집

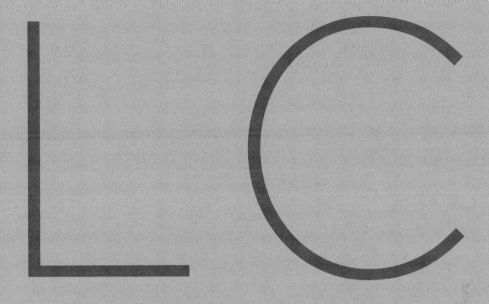

LC

기출 TEST

08

LISTENING TEST

In the Listening test, you will be asked to demonstrate how well you understand spoken English. The entire Listening test will last approximately 45 minutes. There are four parts, and directions are given for each part. You must mark your answers on the separate answer sheet. Do not write your answers in your test book.

PART 1

Directions: For each question in this part, you will hear four statements about a picture in your test book. When you hear the statements, you must select the one statement that best describes what you see in the picture. Then find the number of the question on your answer sheet and mark your answer. The statements will not be printed in your test book and will be spoken only one time.

Statement (C), "They're sitting at a table," is the best description of the picture, so you should select answer (C) and mark it on your answer sheet.

1.

2.

GO ON TO THE NEXT PAGE ➡

TEST 8

3.

4.

5.

6.

GO ON TO THE NEXT PAGE

TEST 8

PART 2

Directions: You will hear a question or statement and three responses spoken in English. They will not be printed in your test book and will be spoken only one time. Select the best response to the question or statement and mark the letter (A), (B), or (C) on your answer sheet.

7. Mark your answer on your answer sheet.

8. Mark your answer on your answer sheet.

9. Mark your answer on your answer sheet.

10. Mark your answer on your answer sheet.

11. Mark your answer on your answer sheet.

12. Mark your answer on your answer sheet.

13. Mark your answer on your answer sheet.

14. Mark your answer on your answer sheet.

15. Mark your answer on your answer sheet.

16. Mark your answer on your answer sheet.

17. Mark your answer on your answer sheet.

18. Mark your answer on your answer sheet.

19. Mark your answer on your answer sheet.

20. Mark your answer on your answer sheet.

21. Mark your answer on your answer sheet.

22. Mark your answer on your answer sheet.

23. Mark your answer on your answer sheet.

24. Mark your answer on your answer sheet.

25. Mark your answer on your answer sheet.

26. Mark your answer on your answer sheet.

27. Mark your answer on your answer sheet.

28. Mark your answer on your answer sheet.

29. Mark your answer on your answer sheet.

30. Mark your answer on your answer sheet.

31. Mark your answer on your answer sheet.

Directions: You will hear some conversations between two or more people. You will be asked to answer three questions about what the speakers say in each conversation. Select the best response to each question and mark the letter (A), (B), (C), or (D) on your answer sheet. The conversations will not be printed in your test book and will be spoken only one time.

32. Where do the speakers work?

(A) At a hotel
(B) At an art gallery
(C) At a hardware store
(D) At a travel agency

33. Why was a building temporarily closed?

(A) To take inventory
(B) To host an event
(C) To complete a renovation
(D) To celebrate a holiday

34. What is the man going to do next?

(A) Post some flyers
(B) Send customers an e-mail
(C) Place a food order
(D) Contact the maintenance department

35. What are the speakers planning?

(A) A company dinner
(B) A conference schedule
(C) An upcoming trip
(D) A factory inspection

36. What does the woman suggest?

(A) Inviting a guest speaker
(B) Reserving a different venue
(C) Checking a budget
(D) Postponing a party

37. What does the woman say will be provided?

(A) Name tags
(B) A city tour
(C) Transportation
(D) Entertainment

38. What are the speakers mainly discussing?

(A) A store sign
(B) A Web site
(C) Some uniforms
(D) Some business cards

39. What suggestion does the man make?

(A) Adding display racks
(B) Giving a demonstration
(C) Researching some suppliers
(D) Advertising a business' hours

40. What does Ana offer to do?

(A) Lead a training session
(B) Greet a client
(C) Update a list
(D) Revise an announcement

41. What type of business is the man calling?

(A) A bookstore
(B) A restaurant
(C) A clothing shop
(D) A printing shop

42. What will happen next week?

(A) A class will begin.
(B) A shipment will arrive.
(C) A location will change.
(D) A sale will end.

43. What information does the woman ask for?

(A) A bank account number
(B) A mailing address
(C) A discount code
(D) A telephone number

TEST 8

GO ON TO THE NEXT PAGE

44. What is the woman concerned about?

(A) The quality of some fabric
(B) The price of a shipment
(C) The size of some furniture
(D) The noise from some construction

45. What does the man say his team will do at the woman's house?

(A) Paint a living room
(B) Assemble a product
(C) Take some measurements
(D) Remove some machinery

46. What does the woman ask the man to do?

(A) Resubmit an order form
(B) Send some samples
(C) Go to a different address
(D) Change a delivery date

47. Why does the man want to hire a temporary employee?

(A) To hand out brochures
(B) To design a Web site
(C) To sort through some documents
(D) To pick up some office equipment

48. According to the man, what does the job require?

(A) Sales experience
(B) Public speaking skills
(C) Interior decorating experience
(D) Computer skills

49. What does the man ask the woman to do?

(A) Check a budget
(B) Sign a contract
(C) Brainstorm marketing ideas
(D) Prepare some invoices

50. Where do the speakers most likely work?

(A) At a hotel
(B) At a restaurant
(C) At a convention hall
(D) At an auto repair shop

51. What does the woman say about her car?

(A) She will loan it to a friend.
(B) She does not use it often.
(C) It was recently purchased.
(D) It needs to be fixed.

52. What does the woman mean when she says, "Thursday is my mother's birthday"?

(A) She is inviting the man to a party.
(B) She cannot work on Thursday night.
(C) She has to buy a gift before Thursday.
(D) She forgot to update a calendar.

53. What most likely is the man's position?

(A) A maintenance worker
(B) A government official
(C) An editor
(D) An accountant

54. What do the women do at their company?

(A) They arrange travel.
(B) They provide legal assistance.
(C) They organize training sessions.
(D) They manage company inventory.

55. What does the man ask about?

(A) Free parking
(B) Technical support
(C) Payment options
(D) Printing supplies

56. Which industry do the speakers most likely work in?

(A) Health care
(B) Architecture
(C) Tourism
(D) Fashion

57. What does the woman mean when she says, "My meeting was canceled"?

(A) She cannot answer a question.
(B) She is available to discuss an issue.
(C) She is confused by a schedule change.
(D) She is worried a project will be delayed.

58. What will the woman most likely do next?

(A) Call a vendor
(B) Distribute a questionnaire
(C) Review some designs
(D) Contact some colleagues

59. What is the topic of an upcoming seminar?

(A) Payroll procedures
(B) Videoconferencing tools
(C) Computer upgrades
(D) Password security

60. What aspect of the seminar do the speakers disagree about?

(A) How long it should last
(B) How it should be announced
(C) Whether attendance should be required
(D) Whether refreshments should be served

61. What does the woman want to distribute after the seminar?

(A) A survey
(B) A manual
(C) Some paychecks
(D) Some hardware

Community Center Spring Activities 6:00–8:00 P.M.		
Monday Pottery	**Tuesday** Swimming	**Wednesday** Chess
Thursday Basketball		**Friday** Movie night

62. Who most likely is the man?

(A) A fitness coach
(B) A teacher
(C) A medical doctor
(D) A receptionist

63. What does the woman ask the man about?

(A) Requirements for a job
(B) Alternative types of exercise
(C) Available appointment times
(D) Operating hours of a business

64. Look at the graphic. When will the woman probably go to the community center in the spring?

(A) On Tuesdays
(B) On Wednesdays
(C) On Thursdays
(D) On Fridays

TEST 8

GO ON TO THE NEXT PAGE

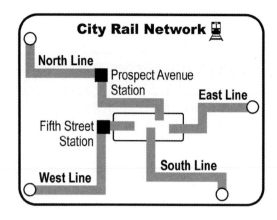

City Rail Network 🚆

North Line
Prospect Avenue Station
East Line
Fifth Street Station
South Line
West Line

Matphase Electronics Model #	On the Head	In the Ear	Noise Reduction
F-12		✓	Fair
A-66	✓		Good
N-48		✓	Excellent
C-94	✓		Excellent

65. What does the man say he is doing tonight?

(A) Taking a flight
(B) Eating in a restaurant
(C) Seeing a performance
(D) Visiting a friend

66. Look at the graphic. Which train line will the man most likely take?

(A) The North Line
(B) The East Line
(C) The South Line
(D) The West Line

67. What does the man ask about a bus?

(A) Whether he needs a different ticket
(B) Whether there are reserved seats
(C) How long the ride will take
(D) How often the bus runs

68. Why is the woman at the store?

(A) To arrange a delivery
(B) To exchange a purchase
(C) To request an instruction manual
(D) To complain about an incorrect charge

69. What is the woman's job?

(A) Jazz musician
(B) Studio photographer
(C) Carpenter
(D) Electrical engineer

70. Look at the graphic. What model does the man recommend?

(A) F-12
(B) A-66
(C) N-48
(D) C-94

PART 4

Directions: You will hear some talks given by a single speaker. You will be asked to answer three questions about what the speaker says in each talk. Select the best response to each question and mark the letter (A), (B), (C), or (D) on your answer sheet. The talks will not be printed in your test book and will be spoken only one time.

71. What field does the listener most likely work in?
    (A) Health care
    (B) Education
    (C) Marketing
    (D) Technology

72. What job requirement does the speaker mention?
    (A) Frequent travel
    (B) Public speaking
    (C) Employee supervision
    (D) Bilingual skills

73. What does the speaker ask the listener to do?
    (A) Attend a trade show
    (B) Contact a new client
    (C) Complete some paperwork
    (D) Suggest a meeting time

74. What event is the speaker discussing?
    (A) A wellness fair
    (B) A luncheon
    (C) A race
    (D) A training session

75. What does the company most likely sell?
    (A) Food
    (B) Footwear
    (C) Clothing
    (D) Electronics

76. What does the speaker ask Leanna to do?
    (A) Conduct a survey
    (B) Select some items
    (C) Visit a location
    (D) Pass out identification badges

77. Who is Anne Pochon?
    (A) A museum director
    (B) A photographer
    (C) A film producer
    (D) A sculptor

78. What does the speaker say will happen in June?
    (A) An art exhibit will be held.
    (B) A company merger will take place.
    (C) A documentary will be released.
    (D) A shop will be renovated.

79. What will the speaker most likely do next?
    (A) Provide directions
    (B) Take some pictures
    (C) Autograph some books
    (D) Interview a guest

80. What does the company sell?
    (A) Chemical products
    (B) Machine parts
    (C) Laboratory equipment
    (D) Home appliances

81. What does the speaker mean when he says, "I went to the convention last year"?
    (A) He does not want to go to an event.
    (B) He is able to help the listeners.
    (C) He is explaining an expense report.
    (D) He disagrees with the listeners' opinions.

82. What does the speaker want the listeners to do when they return?
    (A) Submit some receipts
    (B) Develop an advertising plan
    (C) Give a presentation
    (D) Speak with a supervisor

TEST 8

GO ON TO THE NEXT PAGE

83. Why are the listeners at Rockstone Bank?

(A) To attend a board meeting
(B) To organize a charity event
(C) To open an account
(D) To take part in an internship program

84. What is Ms. Enfield's position?

(A) Customer service representative
(B) Chief executive officer
(C) Branch manager
(D) Loan officer

85. What will Ms. Enfield speak about?

(A) Corporate culture
(B) A company policy
(C) An application process
(D) Career development

86. Where is the talk most likely taking place?

(A) At a supermarket
(B) At a community park
(C) At an art supply store
(D) At a farm

87. What does the speaker remind the listeners to do?

(A) Put belongings in a locker
(B) Fill out a survey
(C) Use sun protection
(D) Read some instructions

88. What does the speaker mean when she says, "all of our flowerpots are twenty percent off"?

(A) She needs the listeners to change some price tags.
(B) She wants the listeners to purchase some merchandise.
(C) She is disappointed that a product did not sell well.
(D) She is surprised by a decision.

89. What is the purpose of the talk?

(A) To offer some training
(B) To revise a handbook
(C) To recommend a hotel
(D) To introduce new staff

90. According to the speaker, what should the listeners remember to do?

(A) Reinstall some software
(B) Complete daily reports
(C) Submit travel vouchers
(D) Save some data

91. Why does the speaker apologize?

(A) His colleague is unavailable.
(B) His computer is malfunctioning.
(C) Some assignments are delayed.
(D) Some requests have been denied.

92. What is the topic of this week's podcast?

(A) The history of eating utensils
(B) The latest cooking trends
(C) Local restaurant reviews
(D) Healthy eating on a budget

93. What does the speaker say will take place next month?

(A) A debut of a new host
(B) A fund-raising event
(C) A live studio broadcast
(D) A trivia contest

94. Why does the speaker say, "That'll only take a minute"?

(A) To correct a misunderstanding
(B) To encourage participation
(C) To ask for permission
(D) To reconsider a suggestion

Customer:	Evergreen Technology
Order:	Business Cards

Quantity	Name
500	Jihoon Lee
1,000	Paola Dias
1,500	Barbara Reynolds
2,000	Mohammed Nasser

COMPANY	BEST FEATURE
Lowz	No equipment charge
Gatepath	Payments from mobile phones
E-buzz	Flexible contracts
MRC	Online customer service

95. Which department does the speaker work in?

(A) Human Resources
(B) Sales
(C) IT
(D) Finance

96. Look at the graphic. Which quantity needs to be changed?

(A) 500
(B) 1,000
(C) 1,500
(D) 2,000

97. What does the speaker say he will do tomorrow?

(A) Provide a logo
(B) Pick up an order
(C) Pay an invoice
(D) Meet with a client

98. What type of business is being launched?

(A) A financial consulting firm
(B) A real estate agency
(C) A restaurant
(D) An electronics store

99. What does the speaker say she is pleased about?

(A) The location of public transportation
(B) The price of some equipment
(C) Some job applications
(D) Some building renovations

100. Look at the graphic. Which company does the speaker want to use?

(A) Lowz
(B) Gatepath
(C) E-buzz
(D) MRC

This is the end of the Listening test.

토익® 정기시험
기출문제집

LC

기출 TEST

09

LISTENING TEST

In the Listening test, you will be asked to demonstrate how well you understand spoken English. The entire Listening test will last approximately 45 minutes. There are four parts, and directions are given for each part. You must mark your answers on the separate answer sheet. Do not write your answers in your test book.

PART 1

Directions: For each question in this part, you will hear four statements about a picture in your test book. When you hear the statements, you must select the one statement that best describes what you see in the picture. Then find the number of the question on your answer sheet and mark your answer. The statements will not be printed in your test book and will be spoken only one time.

Statement (C), "They're sitting at a table," is the best description of the picture, so you should select answer (C) and mark it on your answer sheet.

1.

2.

GO ON TO THE NEXT PAGE ▶

3.

4.

5.

6.

GO ON TO THE NEXT PAGE

PART 2

Directions: You will hear a question or statement and three responses spoken in English. They will not be printed in your test book and will be spoken only one time. Select the best response to the question or statement and mark the letter (A), (B), or (C) on your answer sheet.

7. Mark your answer on your answer sheet.

8. Mark your answer on your answer sheet.

9. Mark your answer on your answer sheet.

10. Mark your answer on your answer sheet.

11. Mark your answer on your answer sheet.

12. Mark your answer on your answer sheet.

13. Mark your answer on your answer sheet.

14. Mark your answer on your answer sheet.

15. Mark your answer on your answer sheet.

16. Mark your answer on your answer sheet.

17. Mark your answer on your answer sheet.

18. Mark your answer on your answer sheet.

19. Mark your answer on your answer sheet.

20. Mark your answer on your answer sheet.

21. Mark your answer on your answer sheet.

22. Mark your answer on your answer sheet.

23. Mark your answer on your answer sheet.

24. Mark your answer on your answer sheet.

25. Mark your answer on your answer sheet.

26. Mark your answer on your answer sheet.

27. Mark your answer on your answer sheet.

28. Mark your answer on your answer sheet.

29. Mark your answer on your answer sheet.

30. Mark your answer on your answer sheet.

31. Mark your answer on your answer sheet.

PART 3

Directions: You will hear some conversations between two or more people. You will be asked to answer three questions about what the speakers say in each conversation. Select the best response to each question and mark the letter (A), (B), (C), or (D) on your answer sheet. The conversations will not be printed in your test book and will be spoken only one time.

32. Where are the speakers?

   (A) At an airport
   (B) At a restaurant
   (C) At a theater
   (D) At a hotel

33. What does the woman ask the man for?

   (A) His reservation number
   (B) His name
   (C) His departure day
   (D) His credit card

34. What will the man most likely do next?

   (A) Park his car
   (B) Upgrade a reservation
   (C) Buy a snack
   (D) Go to the pool

35. Who most likely is the man?

   (A) A painter
   (B) A security guard
   (C) A bank teller
   (D) A property manager

36. What problem does the woman have?

   (A) She found a mistake on a bill.
   (B) She cannot locate a door key.
   (C) An air conditioner is not working.
   (D) An apartment is too noisy.

37. What information does the man ask for?

   (A) An address
   (B) A security code
   (C) A telephone number
   (D) An appointment time

38. Where do the speakers most likely work?

   (A) At a manufacturing plant
   (B) At a delivery company
   (C) At a fitness center
   (D) At a grocery store

39. According to the woman, what does a decision depend on?

   (A) Employee availability
   (B) Government regulations
   (C) A price
   (D) A timeline

40. What does the man say he will do?

   (A) Check delivery dates
   (B) Schedule an inspection
   (C) Contact a supplier
   (D) Test a product

41. What is the man's job?

   (A) University professor
   (B) Newspaper reporter
   (C) Flight attendant
   (D) Tour guide

42. What does the man say he likes about the job?

   (A) Meeting city officials
   (B) Traveling to other countries
   (C) Learning about local history
   (D) Attending special celebrations

43. What does the woman ask the man to do?

   (A) Write an article
   (B) Work more hours
   (C) Train new employees
   (D) Organize an event

TEST 9

GO ON TO THE NEXT PAGE

44. What will be the topic of the woman's article?

(A) Music festivals
(B) Local restaurants
(C) Farmers markets
(D) Sporting events

45. What does the man ask the woman about?

(A) Interviewing some vendors
(B) Reformatting some images
(C) Extending a deadline
(D) Making travel arrangements

46. What does the man mean when he says, "I don't think Elena has any assignments"?

(A) A colleague completes tasks quickly.
(B) A colleague may be available for a job.
(C) An office does not need more staff.
(D) A schedule may be incorrect.

47. Why does the man congratulate the woman?

(A) She recently published a book.
(B) She just received a promotion.
(C) She acquired a major account.
(D) She completed a business course.

48. What does the man ask the woman to do?

(A) Update a reservation
(B) Meet with a new client
(C) Submit a budget report
(D) Give a talk to staff members

49. Where does the woman say she will be going?

(A) To a fund-raising event
(B) To a convention
(C) On a vacation
(D) On a promotional tour

50. Who most likely are the men?

(A) Real estate agents
(B) Interior designers
(C) Marketing executives
(D) Bank managers

51. What does the woman want to discuss first?

(A) A delivery time
(B) A rental fee
(C) Some flooring options
(D) Some machinery upgrades

52. What will the woman most likely do next?

(A) Look at a catalog
(B) Cancel a meeting
(C) Review a receipt
(D) Call a supervisor

53. What is the woman planning to do at two o'clock?

(A) Go to the airport
(B) Receive a shipment
(C) Meet with a customer
(D) Give a workshop

54. What problem is the woman having?

(A) Her log-in information has expired.
(B) Her laptop cable does not work.
(C) Her reservation was not confirmed.
(D) Her mobile phone is missing.

55. What does the man tell the woman to do?

(A) Search in her office
(B) Visit an electronics store
(C) Borrow some equipment
(D) Contact a service team member

56. Where is the conversation taking place?

(A) At a park
(B) At a café
(C) At a furniture store
(D) At a supermarket

57. What does Luisa suggest that the man do?

(A) Open a window
(B) Use a coupon
(C) Visit a plant shop
(D) Extend business hours

58. What does the man ask Luisa for?

(A) A list of prices
(B) A deadline extension
(C) Some coffee
(D) Some photographs

59. What problem does the woman mention?

(A) A product is not selling well.
(B) A position is vacant.
(C) A proposal was not accepted.
(D) A supervisor is busy.

60. Why does the woman say, "He's never done that before"?

(A) To express concern
(B) To request more help
(C) To approve a decision
(D) To offer some praise

61. What does the man say he will do?

(A) Write a report
(B) Conduct an interview
(C) Schedule a meeting
(D) Post an advertisement

```
          Receipt
   Jay's Retail Outlet
   Jacket    $24.00
   Sweater   $13.00
   Scarf     $32.00
   T-shirt   $ 7.00
   Total     $76.00
```

62. Why does the man want to return an item?

(A) It has a stain.
(B) It has a tear.
(C) It is the wrong color.
(D) It is too large.

63. Look at the graphic. Which item does the man want to return?

(A) The jacket
(B) The sweater
(C) The scarf
(D) The T-shirt

64. What does the woman offer to do for the man?

(A) Issue a refund to his credit card
(B) Set up an account for him
(C) Consult with a manager
(D) Call another branch store

GO ON TO THE NEXT PAGE

TEST 9

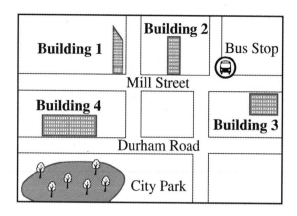

DEPARTURES		
Destination	**Scheduled**	**Status**
Barcelona	9:00 a.m.	40 minutes late
Lisbon	10:30 a.m.	On time
Madrid	11:00 a.m.	55 minutes late
Paris	11:20 a.m.	25 minutes late

65. Who most likely is the woman?

(A) A postal worker
(B) A delivery driver
(C) A repair technician
(D) A building supervisor

66. What problem does the woman mention?

(A) A package has been damaged.
(B) A vehicle is not working.
(C) Some residents are not home.
(D) Some information is missing.

67. Look at the graphic. Where will the woman go next?

(A) To Building 1
(B) To Building 2
(C) To Building 3
(D) To Building 4

68. Look at the graphic. What is the status of the woman's flight?

(A) 40 minutes late
(B) On time
(C) 55 minutes late
(D) 25 minutes late

69. What kind of company do the speakers work for?

(A) A fabric manufacturer
(B) A clothing store
(C) A travel agency
(D) A newspaper publisher

70. What does the man say he is going to do?

(A) Open another bank account
(B) Extend business hours
(C) Review a contract
(D) Change a meeting time

Directions: You will hear some talks given by a single speaker. You will be asked to answer three questions about what the speaker says in each talk. Select the best response to each question and mark the letter (A), (B), (C), or (D) on your answer sheet. The talks will not be printed in your test book and will be spoken only one time.

71. What is the broadcast about?

(A) A fund-raising initiative
(B) A business merger
(C) A new factory
(D) A product launch

72. What benefit is expected for the city of Centerville?

(A) A public park will be expanded.
(B) A hospital will add services.
(C) Roadways will be improved.
(D) Employment will increase.

73. What will the listeners hear next?

(A) A music program
(B) An interview
(C) A sports report
(D) A weather forecast

74. Where does the speaker work?

(A) At a repair shop
(B) At a conference center
(C) In a factory
(D) In a warehouse

75. What does the speaker want to purchase?

(A) Light fixtures
(B) Office furniture
(C) Electronic devices
(D) Employee uniforms

76. What does the speaker imply when she says, "The budget meeting is on Monday, right?"

(A) She wants to participate in a discussion.
(B) She wants to meet some new employees.
(C) She hopes a request will be approved quickly.
(D) She knows that the listener will be unavailable.

77. What type of event is the announcement about?

(A) A music contest
(B) A press conference
(C) A food festival
(D) A government election

78. Why are the listeners encouraged to download an application?

(A) To look at a menu
(B) To cast a vote
(C) To get a map
(D) To check a schedule

79. What does the speaker say volunteers will receive?

(A) A water bottle
(B) A meal coupon
(C) Special seating
(D) Free transportation

80. What kind of merchandise does the company produce?

(A) Eyewear
(B) Footwear
(C) Furniture
(D) Electronics

81. According to the speaker, what do consumers want?

(A) Lower prices
(B) Better packaging
(C) More color selections
(D) More-comfortable designs

82. What information will be e-mailed to the listeners?

(A) An employee survcy
(B) An inventory list
(C) Some product specifications
(D) Some group assignments

GO ON TO THE NEXT PAGE

83. What event is the listener attending soon?

(A) A community fund-raiser
(B) A trade show
(C) A film festival
(D) A sports competition

84. Why does the speaker say, "There's usually a place to stay in Springfield"?

(A) To confirm a reservation
(B) To reject a suggestion
(C) To give directions
(D) To offer a solution

85. What requires a manager's approval?

(A) A conference presentation
(B) A catering request
(C) An equipment purchase
(D) A rental car agreement

86. Who most likely are the listeners?

(A) Construction workers
(B) Park rangers
(C) Gardeners
(D) Architects

87. What will the group do outside?

(A) Measure a plot of land
(B) Clear some trails
(C) Take some photographs
(D) Learn about some equipment

88. What will happen at the end of the day?

(A) Supplies will be collected.
(B) Work schedules will be created.
(C) Certificates will be distributed.
(D) Books will be ordered.

89. Where does the speaker work?

(A) At a furniture store
(B) At a medical clinic
(C) At a fitness center
(D) At a travel agency

90. According to the speaker, what will happen this morning?

(A) Some items will be delivered.
(B) Some workshops will be held.
(C) A building will be inspected.
(D) An article will be published.

91. Why does the speaker need a volunteer?

(A) To order office supplies
(B) To organize a filing system
(C) To distribute some brochures
(D) To schedule some appointments

92. Where does the speaker work?

(A) At a farm
(B) At a factory
(C) At a television station
(D) At a repair shop

93. What does the speaker imply when she says, "all the machines are already running"?

(A) Some instructions were not followed.
(B) It is too late to change an assignment.
(C) A project deadline will be met.
(D) Extra help will not be needed.

94. What is the speaker concerned about?

(A) Misplacing a manual
(B) Exceeding a budget
(C) Breaking a contract
(D) Wasting materials

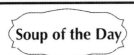

Soup of the Day

Tuesday: French Onion
Wednesday: Tomato Basil
Thursday: Potato and Cheese
Friday: Mixed Seafood

Customer Ratings of Vance Laptop Models

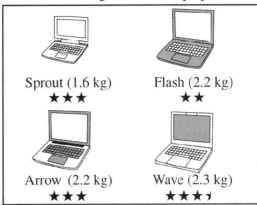

Sprout (1.6 kg)
★★★

Flash (2.2 kg)
★★

Arrow (2.2 kg)
★★★

Wave (2.3 kg)
★★★⟊

95. Look at the graphic. Which soup does the speaker say will be served on two days this week?

(A) French Onion
(B) Tomato Basil
(C) Potato and Cheese
(D) Mixed Seafood

96. Who is Deena Sanchez?

(A) A manager
(B) A server
(C) A customer
(D) A chef

97. What has the speaker placed in the staff lounge?

(A) Uniform shirts
(B) Job applications
(C) A revised menu
(D) A training schedule

98. What will the speaker do next week?

(A) Submit a proposal
(B) Conduct an interview
(C) Move to a new office
(D) Take a business trip

99. According to the speaker, why is Ms. Dubois familiar with Vance Electronics?

(A) She just bought one of their laptops.
(B) She was employed by that company.
(C) She is a purchasing manager.
(D) She read a review in a magazine article.

100. Look at the graphic. Which laptop model does the speaker say she wants to buy?

(A) Sprout
(B) Flash
(C) Arrow
(D) Wave

This is the end of the Listening test.

토익® 정기시험
기출문제집

LC

기출 TEST

10

LISTENING TEST

In the Listening test, you will be asked to demonstrate how well you understand spoken English. The entire Listening test will last approximately 45 minutes. There are four parts, and directions are given for each part. You must mark your answers on the separate answer sheet. Do not write your answers in your test book.

PART 1

Directions: For each question in this part, you will hear four statements about a picture in your test book. When you hear the statements, you must select the one statement that best describes what you see in the picture. Then find the number of the question on your answer sheet and mark your answer. The statements will not be printed in your test book and will be spoken only one time.

Statement (C), "They're sitting at a table," is the best description of the picture, so you should select answer (C) and mark it on your answer sheet.

1.

2.

GO ON TO THE NEXT PAGE

TEST 10

3.

4.

5.

6.

GO ON TO THE NEXT PAGE ➡

TEST 10

PART 2

Directions: You will hear a question or statement and three responses spoken in English. They will not be printed in your test book and will be spoken only one time. Select the best response to the question or statement and mark the letter (A), (B), or (C) on your answer sheet.

7. Mark your answer on your answer sheet.

8. Mark your answer on your answer sheet.

9. Mark your answer on your answer sheet.

10. Mark your answer on your answer sheet.

11. Mark your answer on your answer sheet.

12. Mark your answer on your answer sheet.

13. Mark your answer on your answer sheet.

14. Mark your answer on your answer sheet.

15. Mark your answer on your answer sheet.

16. Mark your answer on your answer sheet.

17. Mark your answer on your answer sheet.

18. Mark your answer on your answer sheet.

19. Mark your answer on your answer sheet.

20. Mark your answer on your answer sheet.

21. Mark your answer on your answer sheet.

22. Mark your answer on your answer sheet.

23. Mark your answer on your answer sheet.

24. Mark your answer on your answer sheet.

25. Mark your answer on your answer sheet.

26. Mark your answer on your answer sheet.

27. Mark your answer on your answer sheet.

28. Mark your answer on your answer sheet.

29. Mark your answer on your answer sheet.

30. Mark your answer on your answer sheet.

31. Mark your answer on your answer sheet.

Directions: You will hear some conversations between two or more people. You will be asked to answer three questions about what the speakers say in each conversation. Select the best response to each question and mark the letter (A), (B), (C), or (D) on your answer sheet. The conversations will not be printed in your test book and will be spoken only one time.

32. Where does the woman say she wants to go?

(A) To an airport
(B) To a beach
(C) To a hotel
(D) To a fitness center

33. Who most likely is the man?

(A) An auto mechanic
(B) A local musician
(C) A security guard
(D) A bus driver

34. Why will the woman return home late?

(A) She is working overtime.
(B) She has a flight delay.
(C) She is attending a concert.
(D) She is eating at a restaurant.

35. Where do the speakers most likely work?

(A) At an appliance manufacturer
(B) At a construction firm
(C) At a grocery store
(D) At an apartment complex

36. What does the woman say she will review?

(A) A budget
(B) A contract
(C) A job posting
(D) An instruction manual

37. What does the man hope to do this afternoon?

(A) Schedule an interview
(B) Arrange a discount
(C) Make a delivery
(D) Print some brochures

38. Who most likely is the man?

(A) A flight attendant
(B) A sales representative
(C) An event organizer
(D) A repair technician

39. Why is Sameera unable to attend a meeting?

(A) Her flight was canceled.
(B) Her car has broken down.
(C) She is on vacation.
(D) She is feeling sick.

40. What does the woman say the man should do before a meeting?

(A) Read some client information
(B) Prepare a contract
(C) Make a dinner reservation
(D) Check some equipment

41. Where do the speakers work?

(A) At a clothing shop
(B) At a photography studio
(C) At a travel agency
(D) At a furniture store

42. Why does the man say, "Coffee shops need a lot of tables and chairs"?

(A) To request assistance
(B) To correct an error
(C) To express disagreement
(D) To make a guess

43. What will the woman do next?

(A) Process an online order
(B) Call the building's property manager
(C) Meet some new neighbors
(D) Fix a broken piece of equipment

TEST 10

GO ON TO THE NEXT PAGE

44. Why does the man apologize?

   (A) He used the wrong entrance.
   (B) He is late for an appointment.
   (C) He forgot to bring identification.
   (D) He lost an order number.

45. What is the man's job?

   (A) Delivery driver
   (B) Electrician
   (C) Journalist
   (D) Security guard

46. Where does the woman direct the man to go?

   (A) To a conference room
   (B) To a security desk
   (C) To a construction site
   (D) To a loading dock

47. Where do the speakers most likely work?

   (A) At an advertising agency
   (B) At an electronics shop
   (C) At a furniture store
   (D) At an assembly plant

48. Why does the woman say, "We've already sold out"?

   (A) To ask for help
   (B) To refuse a request
   (C) To express agreement
   (D) To show concern

49. According to the woman, why is a product popular?

   (A) It has good online reviews.
   (B) It has a lifetime warranty.
   (C) It is being advertised by celebrities.
   (D) It is being sold at a low price.

50. Why are the men at the store?

   (A) To return a defective item
   (B) To purchase a gift
   (C) To publicize a festival
   (D) To apply for a position

51. What hobby is mentioned?

   (A) Hiking
   (B) Swimming
   (C) Skiing
   (D) Cycling

52. What does the woman recommend?

   (A) Finalizing a schedule
   (B) Consulting a return policy
   (C) Getting a membership
   (D) Downloading a map

53. Why are the speakers traveling?

   (A) To attend a conference
   (B) To train some employees
   (C) To meet a client
   (D) To open a new business location

54. What does the man say he will do during the flight?

   (A) Update a travel itinerary
   (B) Edit some presentation slides
   (C) Proofread a contract
   (D) Review some résumés

55. What will the speakers most likely do when they land?

   (A) Check in to a hotel
   (B) Eat at a restaurant
   (C) Board another flight
   (D) Go to an office building

56. Where most likely are the speakers?

(A) In a computer store
(B) In a recording studio
(C) In a medical clinic
(D) In an electrical supply shop

57. What are the speakers mainly discussing?

(A) A work schedule
(B) A recent illness
(C) Some pricing options
(D) Some maintenance problems

58. What does the woman say the men should do?

(A) Contact a manager
(B) Complete a form
(C) Pay a bill
(D) Provide some identification

59. What type of business do the speakers most likely operate?

(A) A cooking school
(B) A kitchen supply store
(C) A dairy farm
(D) A specialty bakery

60. How does the woman want to reduce expenses?

(A) By relocating a business
(B) By shortening operating hours
(C) By using local suppliers
(D) By purchasing in bulk

61. What is the man concerned about?

(A) A change may affect product quality.
(B) A new recipe has not been successful.
(C) An ingredient is no longer being sold.
(D) A competing business is expanding.

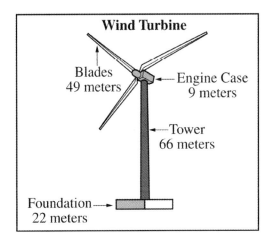

62. What are the speakers mainly discussing?

(A) An inspection of a facility
(B) Transportation of some parts
(C) A revised government policy
(D) Some upcoming road construction

63. What does the man say he will do tomorrow?

(A) Calculate a distance
(B) Adjust a budget
(C) Talk to local officials
(D) Print a permit

64. Look at the graphic. According to the speakers, what will be shipped next?

(A) The engine case
(B) The tower
(C) The foundation
(D) The blades

GO ON TO THE NEXT PAGE

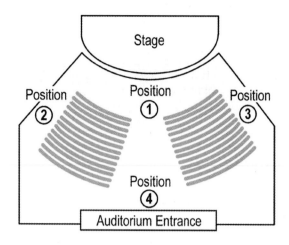

Location	Available Bicycles
65 Elm St.	1
2 Peach St.	4
41 Ames Ave.	3
7 Edson Rd.	2

65. What event are the speakers preparing for?

(A) A professional conference
(B) A political debate
(C) An awards ceremony
(D) A musical concert

66. What was the man asked to do?

(A) Collect tickets
(B) Leave empty rows near the stage
(C) Set up some extra equipment
(D) Pass out programs

67. Look at the graphic. Where will the man most likely be working during the event?

(A) At Position 1
(B) At Position 2
(C) At Position 3
(D) At Position 4

68. What does the woman say about the clients?

(A) Their flight was delayed.
(B) Their contract has not been signed.
(C) They prefer to try a seafood restaurant.
(D) They want to visit museums.

69. What does the man suggest doing?

(A) Updating an event calendar
(B) Trying some local food
(C) Taking a bus tour
(D) Making reservations

70. Look at the graphic. Which location will the speakers go to?

(A) 65 Elm St.
(B) 2 Peach St.
(C) 41 Ames Ave.
(D) 7 Edson Rd.

Directions: You will hear some talks given by a single speaker. You will be asked to answer three questions about what the speaker says in each talk. Select the best response to each question and mark the letter (A), (B), (C), or (D) on your answer sheet. The talks will not be printed in your test book and will be spoken only one time.

71. Where is the announcement being made?

    (A) At a museum
    (B) At a restaurant
    (C) At a bus station
    (D) At a shopping mall

72. What is being offered for free?

    (A) Exhibit passes
    (B) Headphones
    (C) Food samples
    (D) Decorative trees

73. According to the speaker, what will happen next week?

    (A) A road will be closed.
    (B) A menu will change.
    (C) A documentary will be screened.
    (D) A holiday sale will end.

74. Who most likely is Rita Perez?

    (A) A travel agent
    (B) An author
    (C) A librarian
    (D) A news reporter

75. Why is the speaker happy for Rita Perez?

    (A) She won a contest.
    (B) She received a promotion.
    (C) She has become successful.
    (D) She will travel abroad.

76. What does the speaker request that the listeners do?

    (A) Silence their phones
    (B) Take their seats
    (C) Ask questions
    (D) Make a purchase

77. Who most likely are the listeners?

    (A) Laboratory technicians
    (B) Doctors
    (C) Telecommunication specialists
    (D) Software designers

78. What does the speaker imply when she says, "they spent fifteen minutes less than usual completing reports each shift"?

    (A) A product is effective.
    (B) A deadline was extended.
    (C) Some tasks have been reassigned.
    (D) Some staff members are not being careful.

79. What will the listeners do next?

    (A) Tour a facility
    (B) Review some charts
    (C) Enjoy some refreshments
    (D) Watch a product demonstration

80. Where does the speaker work?

    (A) At a health food store
    (B) At a dentist's office
    (C) At a fitness center
    (D) At a pharmacy

81. Why does the speaker say, "we will be short staffed from four to five due to employee training"?

    (A) To ask the listener to work an additional shift
    (B) To encourage the listener to come at a different time
    (C) To complain about a decision
    (D) To refuse a request for time off

82. What does the speaker remind the listener to do?

    (A) Bring Identification
    (B) Pay an overdue bill
    (C) Register online
    (D) Submit a time sheet

GO ON TO THE NEXT PAGE

TEST 10

83. According to the speaker, who is Min-Ah Choi?

(A) A city official
(B) A company president
(C) An office supervisor
(D) A university professor

84. What is the focus of the seminar?

(A) Project management
(B) Computer skills
(C) Financial planning
(D) Product marketing

85. What does the speaker ask the listeners to do?

(A) Sign in online
(B) Pick up a handout
(C) Ask questions
(D) Form small groups

86. Why will a branch office be closed?

(A) Surrounding roads are being repaired.
(B) Sales have recently declined.
(C) The building will be photographed.
(D) The building will undergo renovations.

87. What does the speaker say about conference room B?

(A) It is big enough for a staff meeting.
(B) It will be used as office space.
(C) It has recently been inspected.
(D) It has outdated technology.

88. What will take place on Monday?

(A) A training workshop
(B) A software upgrade
(C) A catered lunch
(D) A facility tour

89. What event is happening in June?

(A) A job fair
(B) A music festival
(C) An art exhibit
(D) A fitness demonstration

90. What kind of prize can the listeners win?

(A) Dinner reservations
(B) Concert tickets
(C) A laptop computer
(D) A musical instrument

91. What does the speaker mean when he says, "all the tickets were gone in an hour"?

(A) The listeners should make a purchase as soon as possible.
(B) The listeners should print more tickets.
(C) An event might begin late.
(D) Some vendors will be pleased.

92. Where most likely are the listeners?

(A) At a bookstore
(B) At a restaurant
(C) At a bus station
(D) At a movie theater

93. What will the speaker mainly talk about today?

(A) Job duties
(B) Health regulations
(C) Sales goals
(D) Customer feedback

94. What does the speaker ask the listeners to do tomorrow?

(A) Arrive early
(B) Wear a specific color
(C) Park in a designated area
(D) Bring photo identification

Original Invoice: Isabel Rodriguez

Initial Assessment	$60
Design Fees	$600
Materials	$2,530
Labor	$1,500

95. What has the speaker's company been working on?

(A) Landscaping a garden
(B) Repairing a garage door
(C) Remodeling a kitchen
(D) Installing solar panels

96. Look at the graphic. Which amount does the speaker say is incorrect?

(A) $60
(B) $600
(C) $2,530
(D) $1,500

97. What does the speaker say he will do tomorrow?

(A) Go to a home repair store
(B) Inspect some equipment
(C) Purchase some new tools
(D) Complete a project

Table Packages

SILVER (Seats 4-6) $12	DELUXE (Seats 8-12) $25
GOLD (Seats 6-8) $20	PREMIUM (Seats 10-16) $35

98. What kind of business is being advertised?

(A) A clothing store
(B) A rental company
(C) A convention center
(D) A furniture manufacturer

99. Look at the graphic. Which table package is available at a discounted price?

(A) Silver
(B) Deluxe
(C) Gold
(D) Premium

100. How can the listeners obtain a discount?

(A) By watching a brief video
(B) By visiting a store location
(C) By speaking with a manager
(D) By entering a promotional code

This is the end of the Listening test.

ANSWER SHEET

ETS® TOEIC 토익® 정기시험 기출문제집

수험번호

응시일자 : 20   년   월   일

성 명
| 한글 |
| 한자 |
| 영자 |

Test 01 (Part 1~4)

Test 02 (Part 1~4)

ANSWER SHEET

ETS® TOEIC® 토익® 정기시험 기출문제집

수험번호						

응시일자 : 20 년 월 일

성명		
	한 글	
	한 자	
	영 자	

Test 03 (Part 1~4)

1	ⓐ ⓑ ⓒ ⓓ	21	ⓐ ⓑ ⓒ	41	ⓐ ⓑ ⓒ ⓓ	61	ⓐ ⓑ ⓒ ⓓ	81	ⓐ ⓑ ⓒ ⓓ
2	ⓐ ⓑ ⓒ ⓓ	22	ⓐ ⓑ ⓒ	42	ⓐ ⓑ ⓒ ⓓ	62	ⓐ ⓑ ⓒ ⓓ	82	ⓐ ⓑ ⓒ ⓓ
3	ⓐ ⓑ ⓒ ⓓ	23	ⓐ ⓑ ⓒ	43	ⓐ ⓑ ⓒ ⓓ	63	ⓐ ⓑ ⓒ ⓓ	83	ⓐ ⓑ ⓒ ⓓ
4	ⓐ ⓑ ⓒ ⓓ	24	ⓐ ⓑ ⓒ	44	ⓐ ⓑ ⓒ ⓓ	64	ⓐ ⓑ ⓒ ⓓ	84	ⓐ ⓑ ⓒ ⓓ
5	ⓐ ⓑ ⓒ ⓓ	25	ⓐ ⓑ ⓒ	45	ⓐ ⓑ ⓒ ⓓ	65	ⓐ ⓑ ⓒ ⓓ	85	ⓐ ⓑ ⓒ ⓓ
6	ⓐ ⓑ ⓒ ⓓ	26	ⓐ ⓑ ⓒ	46	ⓐ ⓑ ⓒ ⓓ	66	ⓐ ⓑ ⓒ ⓓ	86	ⓐ ⓑ ⓒ ⓓ
7	ⓐ ⓑ ⓒ	27	ⓐ ⓑ ⓒ	47	ⓐ ⓑ ⓒ ⓓ	67	ⓐ ⓑ ⓒ ⓓ	87	ⓐ ⓑ ⓒ ⓓ
8	ⓐ ⓑ ⓒ	28	ⓐ ⓑ ⓒ	48	ⓐ ⓑ ⓒ ⓓ	68	ⓐ ⓑ ⓒ ⓓ	88	ⓐ ⓑ ⓒ ⓓ
9	ⓐ ⓑ ⓒ	29	ⓐ ⓑ ⓒ	49	ⓐ ⓑ ⓒ ⓓ	69	ⓐ ⓑ ⓒ ⓓ	89	ⓐ ⓑ ⓒ ⓓ
10	ⓐ ⓑ ⓒ	30	ⓐ ⓑ ⓒ	50	ⓐ ⓑ ⓒ ⓓ	70	ⓐ ⓑ ⓒ ⓓ	90	ⓐ ⓑ ⓒ ⓓ
11	ⓐ ⓑ ⓒ	31	ⓐ ⓑ ⓒ	51	ⓐ ⓑ ⓒ ⓓ	71	ⓐ ⓑ ⓒ ⓓ	91	ⓐ ⓑ ⓒ ⓓ
12	ⓐ ⓑ ⓒ	32	ⓐ ⓑ ⓒ ⓓ	52	ⓐ ⓑ ⓒ ⓓ	72	ⓐ ⓑ ⓒ ⓓ	92	ⓐ ⓑ ⓒ ⓓ
13	ⓐ ⓑ ⓒ	33	ⓐ ⓑ ⓒ ⓓ	53	ⓐ ⓑ ⓒ ⓓ	73	ⓐ ⓑ ⓒ ⓓ	93	ⓐ ⓑ ⓒ ⓓ
14	ⓐ ⓑ ⓒ	34	ⓐ ⓑ ⓒ ⓓ	54	ⓐ ⓑ ⓒ ⓓ	74	ⓐ ⓑ ⓒ ⓓ	94	ⓐ ⓑ ⓒ ⓓ
15	ⓐ ⓑ ⓒ	35	ⓐ ⓑ ⓒ ⓓ	55	ⓐ ⓑ ⓒ ⓓ	75	ⓐ ⓑ ⓒ ⓓ	95	ⓐ ⓑ ⓒ ⓓ
16	ⓐ ⓑ ⓒ	36	ⓐ ⓑ ⓒ ⓓ	56	ⓐ ⓑ ⓒ ⓓ	76	ⓐ ⓑ ⓒ ⓓ	96	ⓐ ⓑ ⓒ ⓓ
17	ⓐ ⓑ ⓒ	37	ⓐ ⓑ ⓒ ⓓ	57	ⓐ ⓑ ⓒ ⓓ	77	ⓐ ⓑ ⓒ ⓓ	97	ⓐ ⓑ ⓒ ⓓ
18	ⓐ ⓑ ⓒ	38	ⓐ ⓑ ⓒ ⓓ	58	ⓐ ⓑ ⓒ ⓓ	78	ⓐ ⓑ ⓒ ⓓ	98	ⓐ ⓑ ⓒ ⓓ
19	ⓐ ⓑ ⓒ	39	ⓐ ⓑ ⓒ ⓓ	59	ⓐ ⓑ ⓒ ⓓ	79	ⓐ ⓑ ⓒ ⓓ	99	ⓐ ⓑ ⓒ ⓓ
20	ⓐ ⓑ ⓒ	40	ⓐ ⓑ ⓒ ⓓ	60	ⓐ ⓑ ⓒ ⓓ	80	ⓐ ⓑ ⓒ ⓓ	100	ⓐ ⓑ ⓒ ⓓ

Test 04 (Part 1~4)

1	ⓐ ⓑ ⓒ ⓓ	21	ⓐ ⓑ ⓒ	41	ⓐ ⓑ ⓒ ⓓ	61	ⓐ ⓑ ⓒ ⓓ	81	ⓐ ⓑ ⓒ ⓓ
2	ⓐ ⓑ ⓒ ⓓ	22	ⓐ ⓑ ⓒ	42	ⓐ ⓑ ⓒ ⓓ	62	ⓐ ⓑ ⓒ ⓓ	82	ⓐ ⓑ ⓒ ⓓ
3	ⓐ ⓑ ⓒ ⓓ	23	ⓐ ⓑ ⓒ	43	ⓐ ⓑ ⓒ ⓓ	63	ⓐ ⓑ ⓒ ⓓ	83	ⓐ ⓑ ⓒ ⓓ
4	ⓐ ⓑ ⓒ ⓓ	24	ⓐ ⓑ ⓒ	44	ⓐ ⓑ ⓒ ⓓ	64	ⓐ ⓑ ⓒ ⓓ	84	ⓐ ⓑ ⓒ ⓓ
5	ⓐ ⓑ ⓒ ⓓ	25	ⓐ ⓑ ⓒ	45	ⓐ ⓑ ⓒ ⓓ	65	ⓐ ⓑ ⓒ ⓓ	85	ⓐ ⓑ ⓒ ⓓ
6	ⓐ ⓑ ⓒ ⓓ	26	ⓐ ⓑ ⓒ	46	ⓐ ⓑ ⓒ ⓓ	66	ⓐ ⓑ ⓒ ⓓ	86	ⓐ ⓑ ⓒ ⓓ
7	ⓐ ⓑ ⓒ	27	ⓐ ⓑ ⓒ	47	ⓐ ⓑ ⓒ ⓓ	67	ⓐ ⓑ ⓒ ⓓ	87	ⓐ ⓑ ⓒ ⓓ
8	ⓐ ⓑ ⓒ	28	ⓐ ⓑ ⓒ	48	ⓐ ⓑ ⓒ ⓓ	68	ⓐ ⓑ ⓒ ⓓ	88	ⓐ ⓑ ⓒ ⓓ
9	ⓐ ⓑ ⓒ	29	ⓐ ⓑ ⓒ	49	ⓐ ⓑ ⓒ ⓓ	69	ⓐ ⓑ ⓒ ⓓ	89	ⓐ ⓑ ⓒ ⓓ
10	ⓐ ⓑ ⓒ	30	ⓐ ⓑ ⓒ	50	ⓐ ⓑ ⓒ ⓓ	70	ⓐ ⓑ ⓒ ⓓ	90	ⓐ ⓑ ⓒ ⓓ
11	ⓐ ⓑ ⓒ	31	ⓐ ⓑ ⓒ	51	ⓐ ⓑ ⓒ ⓓ	71	ⓐ ⓑ ⓒ ⓓ	91	ⓐ ⓑ ⓒ ⓓ
12	ⓐ ⓑ ⓒ	32	ⓐ ⓑ ⓒ ⓓ	52	ⓐ ⓑ ⓒ ⓓ	72	ⓐ ⓑ ⓒ ⓓ	92	ⓐ ⓑ ⓒ ⓓ
13	ⓐ ⓑ ⓒ	33	ⓐ ⓑ ⓒ ⓓ	53	ⓐ ⓑ ⓒ ⓓ	73	ⓐ ⓑ ⓒ ⓓ	93	ⓐ ⓑ ⓒ ⓓ
14	ⓐ ⓑ ⓒ	34	ⓐ ⓑ ⓒ ⓓ	54	ⓐ ⓑ ⓒ ⓓ	74	ⓐ ⓑ ⓒ ⓓ	94	ⓐ ⓑ ⓒ ⓓ
15	ⓐ ⓑ ⓒ	35	ⓐ ⓑ ⓒ ⓓ	55	ⓐ ⓑ ⓒ ⓓ	75	ⓐ ⓑ ⓒ ⓓ	95	ⓐ ⓑ ⓒ ⓓ
16	ⓐ ⓑ ⓒ	36	ⓐ ⓑ ⓒ ⓓ	56	ⓐ ⓑ ⓒ ⓓ	76	ⓐ ⓑ ⓒ ⓓ	96	ⓐ ⓑ ⓒ ⓓ
17	ⓐ ⓑ ⓒ	37	ⓐ ⓑ ⓒ ⓓ	57	ⓐ ⓑ ⓒ ⓓ	77	ⓐ ⓑ ⓒ ⓓ	97	ⓐ ⓑ ⓒ ⓓ
18	ⓐ ⓑ ⓒ	38	ⓐ ⓑ ⓒ ⓓ	58	ⓐ ⓑ ⓒ ⓓ	78	ⓐ ⓑ ⓒ ⓓ	98	ⓐ ⓑ ⓒ ⓓ
19	ⓐ ⓑ ⓒ	39	ⓐ ⓑ ⓒ ⓓ	59	ⓐ ⓑ ⓒ ⓓ	79	ⓐ ⓑ ⓒ ⓓ	99	ⓐ ⓑ ⓒ ⓓ
20	ⓐ ⓑ ⓒ	40	ⓐ ⓑ ⓒ ⓓ	60	ⓐ ⓑ ⓒ ⓓ	80	ⓐ ⓑ ⓒ ⓓ	100	ⓐ ⓑ ⓒ ⓓ

ANSWER SHEET

ETS® TOEIC® 토익 정기시험 기출문제집

수험번호

응시일자 : 20   년   월   일

성명	한글
	한자
	영자

Test 05 (Part 1~4)

1 ~ 100

Test 06 (Part 1~4)

1 ~ 100

ANSWER SHEET

ETS TOEIC 토익 정기시험 기출문제집

수험번호

응시일자 : 20   년   월   일

한글 / 한자 / 영자

성명

Test 07 (Part 1~4)

Test 08 (Part 1~4)

ANSWER SHEET

ETS® TOEIC® 토익® 정기시험 기출문제집

수험번호 | | | | | | |

응시일자 : 20 년 월 일

성명	
한 글	
한 자	
영 자	

Test 09 (Part 1~4)

1	ⓐ ⓑ ⓒ ⓓ	21	ⓐ ⓑ ⓒ	41	ⓐ ⓑ ⓒ ⓓ	61	ⓐ ⓑ ⓒ ⓓ	81	ⓐ ⓑ ⓒ ⓓ
2	ⓐ ⓑ ⓒ ⓓ	22	ⓐ ⓑ ⓒ	42	ⓐ ⓑ ⓒ ⓓ	62	ⓐ ⓑ ⓒ ⓓ	82	ⓐ ⓑ ⓒ ⓓ
3	ⓐ ⓑ ⓒ ⓓ	23	ⓐ ⓑ ⓒ	43	ⓐ ⓑ ⓒ ⓓ	63	ⓐ ⓑ ⓒ ⓓ	83	ⓐ ⓑ ⓒ ⓓ
4	ⓐ ⓑ ⓒ ⓓ	24	ⓐ ⓑ ⓒ	44	ⓐ ⓑ ⓒ ⓓ	64	ⓐ ⓑ ⓒ ⓓ	84	ⓐ ⓑ ⓒ ⓓ
5	ⓐ ⓑ ⓒ ⓓ	25	ⓐ ⓑ ⓒ	45	ⓐ ⓑ ⓒ ⓓ	65	ⓐ ⓑ ⓒ ⓓ	85	ⓐ ⓑ ⓒ ⓓ
6	ⓐ ⓑ ⓒ ⓓ	26	ⓐ ⓑ ⓒ	46	ⓐ ⓑ ⓒ ⓓ	66	ⓐ ⓑ ⓒ ⓓ	86	ⓐ ⓑ ⓒ ⓓ
7	ⓐ ⓑ ⓒ	27	ⓐ ⓑ ⓒ	47	ⓐ ⓑ ⓒ ⓓ	67	ⓐ ⓑ ⓒ ⓓ	87	ⓐ ⓑ ⓒ ⓓ
8	ⓐ ⓑ ⓒ	28	ⓐ ⓑ ⓒ	48	ⓐ ⓑ ⓒ ⓓ	68	ⓐ ⓑ ⓒ ⓓ	88	ⓐ ⓑ ⓒ ⓓ
9	ⓐ ⓑ ⓒ	29	ⓐ ⓑ ⓒ	49	ⓐ ⓑ ⓒ ⓓ	69	ⓐ ⓑ ⓒ ⓓ	89	ⓐ ⓑ ⓒ ⓓ
10	ⓐ ⓑ ⓒ	30	ⓐ ⓑ ⓒ	50	ⓐ ⓑ ⓒ ⓓ	70	ⓐ ⓑ ⓒ ⓓ	90	ⓐ ⓑ ⓒ ⓓ
11	ⓐ ⓑ ⓒ	31	ⓐ ⓑ ⓒ	51	ⓐ ⓑ ⓒ ⓓ	71	ⓐ ⓑ ⓒ ⓓ	91	ⓐ ⓑ ⓒ ⓓ
12	ⓐ ⓑ ⓒ	32	ⓐ ⓑ ⓒ ⓓ	52	ⓐ ⓑ ⓒ ⓓ	72	ⓐ ⓑ ⓒ ⓓ	92	ⓐ ⓑ ⓒ ⓓ
13	ⓐ ⓑ ⓒ	33	ⓐ ⓑ ⓒ ⓓ	53	ⓐ ⓑ ⓒ ⓓ	73	ⓐ ⓑ ⓒ ⓓ	93	ⓐ ⓑ ⓒ ⓓ
14	ⓐ ⓑ ⓒ	34	ⓐ ⓑ ⓒ ⓓ	54	ⓐ ⓑ ⓒ ⓓ	74	ⓐ ⓑ ⓒ ⓓ	94	ⓐ ⓑ ⓒ ⓓ
15	ⓐ ⓑ ⓒ	35	ⓐ ⓑ ⓒ ⓓ	55	ⓐ ⓑ ⓒ ⓓ	75	ⓐ ⓑ ⓒ ⓓ	95	ⓐ ⓑ ⓒ ⓓ
16	ⓐ ⓑ ⓒ	36	ⓐ ⓑ ⓒ ⓓ	56	ⓐ ⓑ ⓒ ⓓ	76	ⓐ ⓑ ⓒ ⓓ	96	ⓐ ⓑ ⓒ ⓓ
17	ⓐ ⓑ ⓒ	37	ⓐ ⓑ ⓒ ⓓ	57	ⓐ ⓑ ⓒ ⓓ	77	ⓐ ⓑ ⓒ ⓓ	97	ⓐ ⓑ ⓒ ⓓ
18	ⓐ ⓑ ⓒ	38	ⓐ ⓑ ⓒ ⓓ	58	ⓐ ⓑ ⓒ ⓓ	78	ⓐ ⓑ ⓒ ⓓ	98	ⓐ ⓑ ⓒ ⓓ
19	ⓐ ⓑ ⓒ	39	ⓐ ⓑ ⓒ ⓓ	59	ⓐ ⓑ ⓒ ⓓ	79	ⓐ ⓑ ⓒ ⓓ	99	ⓐ ⓑ ⓒ ⓓ
20	ⓐ ⓑ ⓒ	40	ⓐ ⓑ ⓒ ⓓ	60	ⓐ ⓑ ⓒ ⓓ	80	ⓐ ⓑ ⓒ ⓓ	100	ⓐ ⓑ ⓒ ⓓ

Test 10 (Part 1~4)

1	ⓐ ⓑ ⓒ ⓓ	21	ⓐ ⓑ ⓒ	41	ⓐ ⓑ ⓒ ⓓ	61	ⓐ ⓑ ⓒ ⓓ	81	ⓐ ⓑ ⓒ ⓓ
2	ⓐ ⓑ ⓒ ⓓ	22	ⓐ ⓑ ⓒ	42	ⓐ ⓑ ⓒ ⓓ	62	ⓐ ⓑ ⓒ ⓓ	82	ⓐ ⓑ ⓒ ⓓ
3	ⓐ ⓑ ⓒ ⓓ	23	ⓐ ⓑ ⓒ	43	ⓐ ⓑ ⓒ ⓓ	63	ⓐ ⓑ ⓒ ⓓ	83	ⓐ ⓑ ⓒ ⓓ
4	ⓐ ⓑ ⓒ ⓓ	24	ⓐ ⓑ ⓒ	44	ⓐ ⓑ ⓒ ⓓ	64	ⓐ ⓑ ⓒ ⓓ	84	ⓐ ⓑ ⓒ ⓓ
5	ⓐ ⓑ ⓒ ⓓ	25	ⓐ ⓑ ⓒ	45	ⓐ ⓑ ⓒ ⓓ	65	ⓐ ⓑ ⓒ ⓓ	85	ⓐ ⓑ ⓒ ⓓ
6	ⓐ ⓑ ⓒ ⓓ	26	ⓐ ⓑ ⓒ	46	ⓐ ⓑ ⓒ ⓓ	66	ⓐ ⓑ ⓒ ⓓ	86	ⓐ ⓑ ⓒ ⓓ
7	ⓐ ⓑ ⓒ	27	ⓐ ⓑ ⓒ	47	ⓐ ⓑ ⓒ ⓓ	67	ⓐ ⓑ ⓒ ⓓ	87	ⓐ ⓑ ⓒ ⓓ
8	ⓐ ⓑ ⓒ	28	ⓐ ⓑ ⓒ	48	ⓐ ⓑ ⓒ ⓓ	68	ⓐ ⓑ ⓒ ⓓ	88	ⓐ ⓑ ⓒ ⓓ
9	ⓐ ⓑ ⓒ	29	ⓐ ⓑ ⓒ	49	ⓐ ⓑ ⓒ ⓓ	69	ⓐ ⓑ ⓒ ⓓ	89	ⓐ ⓑ ⓒ ⓓ
10	ⓐ ⓑ ⓒ	30	ⓐ ⓑ ⓒ	50	ⓐ ⓑ ⓒ ⓓ	70	ⓐ ⓑ ⓒ ⓓ	90	ⓐ ⓑ ⓒ ⓓ
11	ⓐ ⓑ ⓒ	31	ⓐ ⓑ ⓒ	51	ⓐ ⓑ ⓒ ⓓ	71	ⓐ ⓑ ⓒ ⓓ	91	ⓐ ⓑ ⓒ ⓓ
12	ⓐ ⓑ ⓒ	32	ⓐ ⓑ ⓒ ⓓ	52	ⓐ ⓑ ⓒ ⓓ	72	ⓐ ⓑ ⓒ ⓓ	92	ⓐ ⓑ ⓒ ⓓ
13	ⓐ ⓑ ⓒ	33	ⓐ ⓑ ⓒ ⓓ	53	ⓐ ⓑ ⓒ ⓓ	73	ⓐ ⓑ ⓒ ⓓ	93	ⓐ ⓑ ⓒ ⓓ
14	ⓐ ⓑ ⓒ	34	ⓐ ⓑ ⓒ ⓓ	54	ⓐ ⓑ ⓒ ⓓ	74	ⓐ ⓑ ⓒ ⓓ	94	ⓐ ⓑ ⓒ ⓓ
15	ⓐ ⓑ ⓒ	35	ⓐ ⓑ ⓒ ⓓ	55	ⓐ ⓑ ⓒ ⓓ	75	ⓐ ⓑ ⓒ ⓓ	95	ⓐ ⓑ ⓒ ⓓ
16	ⓐ ⓑ ⓒ	36	ⓐ ⓑ ⓒ ⓓ	56	ⓐ ⓑ ⓒ ⓓ	76	ⓐ ⓑ ⓒ ⓓ	96	ⓐ ⓑ ⓒ ⓓ
17	ⓐ ⓑ ⓒ	37	ⓐ ⓑ ⓒ ⓓ	57	ⓐ ⓑ ⓒ ⓓ	77	ⓐ ⓑ ⓒ ⓓ	97	ⓐ ⓑ ⓒ ⓓ
18	ⓐ ⓑ ⓒ	38	ⓐ ⓑ ⓒ ⓓ	58	ⓐ ⓑ ⓒ ⓓ	78	ⓐ ⓑ ⓒ ⓓ	98	ⓐ ⓑ ⓒ ⓓ
19	ⓐ ⓑ ⓒ	39	ⓐ ⓑ ⓒ ⓓ	59	ⓐ ⓑ ⓒ ⓓ	79	ⓐ ⓑ ⓒ ⓓ	99	ⓐ ⓑ ⓒ ⓓ
20	ⓐ ⓑ ⓒ	40	ⓐ ⓑ ⓒ ⓓ	60	ⓐ ⓑ ⓒ ⓓ	80	ⓐ ⓑ ⓒ ⓓ	100	ⓐ ⓑ ⓒ ⓓ